LOVE IS THE WAY

LOVE
IS THE WAY

*Holding on to Hope
in Troubling Times*

BISHOP MICHAEL CURRY

with Sara Grace

HODDER

First published in Great Britain in 2020 by Hodder & Stoughton
An Hachette UK company

Published by arrangement with Avery, an imprint of Penguin Publishing
Group, a division of Penguin Random House LLC.
First published in the United States in 2020.

This paperback edition first published in 2022

1

Book design by Katy Reigel

A CIP catalogue record for this title is available from the British Library

Paperback ISBN 978 1 529 33735 8
eBook ISBN 978 1 529 33734 1

Typeset in Warnock Pro
Printed and bound in Great Britain by Clays Ltd, Elcograf S.p.A.

Hodder & Stoughton policy is to use papers that are natural, renewable and
recyclable products and made from wood grown in sustainable forests. The
logging and manufacturing processes are expected to conform to the
environmental regulations of the country of origin.

Hodder & Stoughton Ltd
Carmelite House
50 Victoria Embankment
London EC4Y 0DZ

www.hodderfaith.com

To the Ancestors.

*To my wife, Sharon; my sister, Sharon;
and my daughters, Rachel and Elizabeth.*

To Josie Robbins.

To the Curry and Strayhorne families.

*To all of my friends and colleagues
who are witness to what love is
and why it really matters.*

Contents

Introduction

ONE OF MY daughters asked me as I was working on this book, "What are you writing about?" I answered, "Some of what I've learned from faith, family, community, and ancestors."

She said, "So you're writing about life lessons?"

"I guess so, yes," I replied.

I don't think of my life as particularly extraordinary, unusual, or even interesting, or at least not any more so than anyone else's. But then there's the wise Frederick Buechner quote from his book *Now and Then: A Memoir of Vocation*: "Listen to your life. See it for the fathomless mystery it is. In the boredom and pain of it, no less than in the excitement and gladness: touch, taste, smell your way to the holy and hidden heart of it, because in the last analysis all moments are key moments, and life itself is grace."

Buechner is actually right about anyone's life, if you listen. *Love Is the Way*, then, is a journey into the holy and hidden heart of my own life—those people and experiences that led to my conviction that the way of love can change each of us, and all of us, for the better.

I was born, grew up, and came of age in the United States of the 1950s, '60s, and early '70s. My sister, Sharon, and I were both born in Chicago, where our father pastored an Episcopal church, St. Simon the Cyrenian, in Maywood. We moved to Buffalo, New York, when I was three. There we grew up in the African American community of East Buffalo—not just raised in the community but by it. Like many in our community, we lived in the urban North, but our roots were deep in the soil of the rural South, and deeper still in time in the ancient soil of sub-Saharan West Africa.

My grandparents came from eastern North Carolina on my mother's side, and on my father's side, from rural Alabama, a place the family referred to as Midway, located midway between Birmingham and Montgomery. They had names like Nellie and Hezekiah, Theotis Calhoun and Carrie Estelle. They weren't unusual. They were part of what the Swedish economist Gunnar Myrdal called "the Great Migration," one of the largest movements in human history, which is powerfully chronicled in Isabel Wilkerson's *The Warmth of Other Suns*.

They migrated from the South; more accurately, they fled the South, not unlike migrants, immigrants, and refugees of all human generations, as far back as the Hebrews fleeing famine and settling as immigrants in Egypt, or

Mary, Joseph, and the baby Jesus generations later fleeing persecution in Palestine and finding refuge in Egypt.

They fled separate bathrooms and water fountains. They fled separate and unequal schools. They fled being segregated, separated, cast down, and cast out. They fled the place where old men were called *boy* and old women were treated with disrespect. They fled the terror of hooded night riders and legalized lynchings and the subtle slavery of sharecropping.

These ancestors fought in the Great War, World War I, to make the world "safe for democracy." My wife, Sharon, proudly has the discharge papers of Troy Rufus Clement, her grandfather, who fought in that war to make the world safe for democracy. But when he came home to North Carolina, that democracy didn't apply to him.

They fought again in World War II, in segregated units, to stop oppression and injustice and evil overseas. And yet again, it didn't apply to them when they came back home. I remember hearing my family on my father's side, in the empire of rural Alabama, talking about how Nazi prisoners of war were treated better than they were.

And yet, in spite of it, they believed in America, in its ideals of freedom and equality, with liberty and justice for *all*. They believed in the dream of America. So they proudly sang the national anthem, "The Star-Spangled Banner," and James Weldon Johnson and J. Rosamond Johnson's Negro national anthem, "Lift Every Voice and Sing."

They loved America and taught us to love America—to work to change it for the good, not just for our people but for all the children of God, no matter their color, class, caste, or creed. All! They loved America in spite of the fact that America didn't love them. My father used to say that his work in the community for civil and human rights was so that his children and others like them would not have to live as second-class citizens.

They taught us, and would say often, quoting the old King James Version of the Bible, that "God is no respecter of persons." And "the Lord God made of one blood all the peoples of the earth to dwell upon the face of the earth." In other words, God doesn't discriminate. The love of God, which is the source of and key to life, is an equal-opportunity employer.

I remember them saying over and over again, possibly quoting Booker T. Washington, "Never let anyone drag you so low as to make you hate them." It is only by discipline and "mobilized love," as my colleague Bishop Mariann Budde of Washington calls it, that we shall all overcome.

So while this book is about me, it's really about the folk who raised me, and the community and church that formed me. First and foremost, they taught that the way of Jesus is the way of love. And that the way of love is the only way to freedom.

They were not at all unusual in African American communities, longing and laboring for freedom, as folk said in those days. In many respects they were representative of the most profound yearning of the human heart: the universal hope for a better life and a better world.

Chaos or Community

The purpose of this book is to explain what the way of love looks like, even as we walk it in a world that feels at times closer to a nightmare than to the dream. The way of love is how we stay decent during indecent times. It's for all of us who are sitting, looking around at the world, at our leaders, saying, "Something has gone very wrong." It's for those who are fighting hard for a better world, and feeling very, very tired.

Dr. Martin Luther King—who, besides my father and grandmother, is the human most responsible for my wearing the collar today—wisely said, "We must learn to live together as brothers or perish together as fools."[1] He was right in the late 1960s when he said it, and it's right in this twenty-first century. We can no longer afford the demonic luxury of bigotry or the false hope of hatred. We must learn to live together as brothers and sisters, all of us children of God. As Dr. King also often said in this regard, we have two choices before us, chaos or community.

The Bible says, "Choose this day who you will serve." I believe, and I suspect most of you do, too, that we must choose community—the human community, in community with all of creation. This is the beloved community of God. This is what the late lay theologian Verna Dozier and Archbishop Desmond Tutu have often called "the dream of God." And love—unselfish, sacrificial, unconditional, and liberating love—is the way, frankly the only way, to realize God's dream of the beloved community, on earth as it is in heaven. It's the only thing that can, and that ever will, make the world a better place.

I learned that from the people who raised me, and so I learned it as they did, from the life and teachings of Jesus of Nazareth, whose way is this kind of love. But love is an equal-opportunity employer. It is a gift of God, flowing from the very heart of creation. It cannot be claimed by any single religion or philosophy or person. "Beloved, let us love one another, because love is from God; everyone who loves is born of God and knows God. Whoever does not love does not know God, for God is love." That's not my opinion—that's from the Bible, 1 John 4:7–8.

Love creates room and space for others, "the other," to be. In the New Testament, in a section of John's Gospel, Jesus says, "In my Father's house there are many dwelling places."[2] The poetry of the King James Version makes it even more powerful: "In my Father's house are many mansions." It's not an accident that when Jesus teaches about the way of love, he speaks of the kingdom of God as the most spacious reality imaginable. That insight led African slaves of America's antebellum South to create and sing a spiritual:

There's plenty good room,
Plenty good room,
Plenty good room in my Father's kingdom;
Plenty good room,
Plenty good room,
Choose your seat and sit down.

There's truly room for everyone. This, too, I learned from my elders. One summer we were visiting my maternal grandma at her family home in Winton, North Carolina. Each day they opened the doors and sent us out with the words "Go on out and play. Just stay away from the creek." Of course, you know we always went straight to the creek. One day, though, we had other plans. Some kids in the neighborhood told us about a revival coming to town that evening. So after supper we got on our bikes and went. A giant tent had been thrown up in an empty lot. We'd been told it was a revival, but we didn't understand the word well enough to ask the obvious question: A revival of *what*?

The tent was packed full. We were Episcopalian kids. Church, as we knew it, was politely sitting in the pews, quietly saying and reading prayers, standing to sing hymns, and then sitting quietly for a few wise, considered words from the pulpit. Nobody got excited, or if they did, they didn't display it in those days.

But at this tent revival, more Pentecostal than Baptist, the preacher shouted. Folk spoke in unknown tongues, people got saved, and some even got healed. Amen! Hallelujah! Glory!

We went home howling with laughter. Outside my aunt's house, we were making fun, imitating the preacher and the congregation. We rolled around in the dust, saving each other's souls, in complete hysterics. Grandma just watched. We didn't know it yet, but we were busted. Come Sunday supper, she sat us down and told us how things were going to be going forward. "You don't laugh at anybody else's religion. You respect the Lord however he comes."

Living Love's Questions

So here I am, fifty years later, the presiding bishop of The Episcopal Church, encouraging a revival of love as a way to a liberating and life-giving relationship with God, with others, with all God's creation on the planet we call Earth.

But this goes far beyond a denomination, and beyond Christianity. This is the revival of love as the guide for living; for relationships; for leaders; for our individual and collective spiritual, material, and physical well-being. I understand Grandma's message today better than ever. Only God is God. None of us are. While we must be discerning, love is the ultimate criteria for that. Our job isn't to tell anybody how they should work out their relationship with the living God. Our job is to love, and in the case of

Christians, to witness to the way of love that came to us from Jesus's teachings.

I had no idea that one day I would receive a call from the archbishop of Canterbury, calling on behalf of Prince Harry and Meghan Markle, now the Duke and Duchess of Sussex: If I were to be asked, might I be available to preach at their upcoming wedding? I could not have dreamed or imagined that invitation, which gave me the opportunity to take this message of love to the world.

What I learned that day, preaching in the presence of Her Majesty, The Queen—and, it turned out, an audience of billions—is that we are hungry for love. No matter our state or condition. Beyond our national identities and loyalties, beyond our political sympathies and ideologies, beyond our religious and spiritual convictions and commitments, there is a universal hunger at the heart of every human being: to love and to be loved. It connects all people of faith, hope, and good will.

That love is truly ecumenical, truly universal. That love knows no borders, no limitations, no divisions or differences of race, class, caste, nationality, ethnic origin, political affiliation, or religious conviction. That love can break down every barrier that blocks the way to the realization of God's dream of the beloved community.

In 2019, when I wrote this book, I was on the road easily 75 percent of the time. During one typical month, I went on seven trips—to England, West Virginia, Michigan, Alabama, New York, Wisconsin, and South Dakota. In these travels, I meet a lot of people, and they ask me a lot of questions. I'm sure you have a few yourself. This book is roughly organized according to the events and lessons learned in my own life. But each chapter also addresses a question that I've been asked by people I've met in churches, at public events, on TV, and even in airports.

1. What is love?
2. How do I find God's love?
3. How do I find the energy to keep loving when the world seems to be going the other way?
4. Can love *really* change the world?
5. Won't loving everybody make me a doormat?
6. I'm just a regular person, so how can my love have an impact?
7. I'm told to love my neighbor, but who *is* my neighbor?
8. What if love reveals me to be a hypocrite?
9. Do I have to love even my enemy?
10. How can love overcome what divides us and move us forward together?
11. Does love mean avoiding politics?
12. How can love make "E Pluribus Unum" real in America without erasing anybody?

I have faith in God. I also have faith in us. We can get this right. The world has changed before, and it can change again, for the better. And we can find peace and joy in our hearts in the interim, even as we carry on the struggle for a humane, just, and peaceful world ruled by love.

However the future unfolds—whatever the detours, the trials, the troubles, the goal, the zenith, or the pain—we shall overcome, not for ourselves alone, but for the entire human family.

CHAPTER 1

What Is This Thing
Called Love?

Question: What is love?

IN MY OWN life, love has had so many, many faces, but among the boldest is the face of Josie Robbins. Josie, who's eighty-five years old as I write this and still in my life, was one of the people who took care of me and my sister when my mother passed away after a long illness. When my father first asked her to help take care of us during Mommy's illness and after, she wasn't a longtime family friend. She was just a lady who stopped by his church some Sundays to drop off her neighbor's child before going to her own Baptist church. But she heard about our family's situation and asked, "How can I help?" Soon thereafter my father nervously welcomed her into our house and led her to the spare bedroom, where both twin beds were covered with clothes that my father had managed to wash but not iron. Josie had never been in our house, hadn't met the children who wore most of those clothes, but she ironed every single garment with love. A little later my father called: He was running late, could she give his kids lunch? We, who had been instructed to play upstairs and not bother Ms. Robbins, came running down to meet the woman who would eventually be a surrogate mother to us. I can't remember the day, but she says that after lunch, I pulled up a chair next to her ironing board and didn't stop talking until the moment she finished and left.

Moved by love, Josie jumped in with both arms and never let go. She would take me and my sister on the bus to the W. T. Grant store in downtown Buffalo so that we could head straight for the parakeets and hamsters, like we had done with Mommy. She made the hurt go away. She was the only person my tender-headed sister ever let wash and braid her hair, because no one else in this world was so patient and careful not to pull. She had dinner with us so many nights, and over the years was present at all our family events and big days—from my high school, college, and seminary graduations, to weddings, ordinations, births and baptisms, and on and on and on.

Josie Robbins is what love looks like. It's important that we define the word *love* here with clarity, because these days we use the word to mean so many things. We might use it to talk about how we feel about our spouse or significant other, or about our children . . . or about our new sofa. The love I'm talking about isn't love on a Valentine's Day card. Those are nice, but they're not what I have in mind when I say that love is the only thing that can save the planet.

Many languages have several words for love, to encompass all the different kinds and dimensions. The three most frequently used in Koine Greek, the language of the New Testament, are *eros, philia*, and *agape. Eros* is romantic or sexual love. Our English word *erotic* comes from that. Eros is what Valentine's Day is about. *Philia* is fraternal or brotherly love, which is why the city of Philadelphia is called the City of Brotherly Love. And finally, there is *agape*, which is love for the other—sacrificial love that seeks the good and well-being of others, of society, of the world.

Unfortunately in English we have only the one word, *love,* for everything from telenovelas to Mother Teresa. And so the different dimensions and nuances have all been muddled together, which has obscured love's true power to instigate a better world. Agape, love that looks outward, is the love that I'm most interested in.

You may not have heard the Greek word before, but you've experienced agape. Think about someone who impacted your life for the good. Someone who stood by you, pushed you, believed in you, maybe even sacrificed for you. Odds are they weren't doing it because it served them. They were doing it because they cared about you. Because they wanted life's sweetness to open wide to you.

Love is a firm commitment to act for the well-being of someone other than yourself. It can be personal or political, individual or communal, intimate or public. Love will not be segregated to the private, personal precincts of life.

Love, as I read it in the Bible, is ubiquitous. It affects all aspects of life.

What I didn't know as a kid was that Josie Robbins's love, shared so generously with my family, had changed many other lives as well. Josie was a principal at St. Augustine's School, a high school for pregnant and parenting teens. She had walked in thinking that it was a summer position—and never left. In the 1960s, when girls got pregnant in Buffalo, like most other places, they weren't allowed to stay in school. But Josie and St. Augustine's, which became Fulton Academic Complex with the support of the public school system, picked them back up. They gave them the chance at a better future for themselves and their children. Because of Josie, thousands of girls got their diplomas and the pride of walking the stage to graduate with their class. The school is now closed—partly because Josie retired, but also because Josie and others advocated until the day the public schools stopped punishing those mothers who were still children themselves, so they could get their education and keep their dignity.

An oft-quoted passage in the New Testament says, "God so loved the world that he gave his only son." The Greek word used by the New Testament writer for the word *love* is *agape*. And the Greek word used for *world* is *kosmos*, but what it really means is *"everything"*—"everything that is." *Kosmos* is what the spiritual is talking about when it says of God, "He's got the whole world in his hands."

God so loved the world that he "gave." God gave. God did not take. God gave. That's agape. That's love. And love such as that is the way to the heart of God, the heart of each other. It is the way to a new world that looks something more like God's dream for us and all creation, what Dante spoke of as "the love that moves the sun and stars."

Love Is Rules for Living

I've officiated more than a few weddings in forty years as a preacher. In the course of preparing couples for marriage and for the actual wedding, I ask them to select a passage of scripture to be read in the service. Nine times out of ten they choose 1 Corinthians 13, St. Paul's great guidelines for love. I've almost gotten them memorized by now. They're famous enough that you might have, too. The passage begins with these words:

> If I speak in the tongues of men and of angels, but have not love, I am a noisy gong or a clanging cymbal. And if I have prophetic powers, and understand all mysteries and all knowledge, and if I have all faith, so as to remove mountains, but have not love, I am nothing. If I give away all I have, and if I deliver my body to be burned, but have not love, I gain nothing.
>
> Love is patient; love is kind;
> love is not envious or boastful or arrogant or rude.

It does not insist on its own way; it is not irritable or resentful;

it does not rejoice in wrongdoing, but rejoices in the truth.

It bears all things, believes all things, hopes all things, endures all things.

Love never ends.

Paul gets it. But it's easy for us today to miss it, having limited the use of *love* as we have to weddings and babies. Because here's the catch. When Paul said those beautiful words about love, he wasn't at a wedding. He wasn't giving advice to a couple of young lovers about how to make a marriage work, though his advice is great for that, too. Paul broke love down so eloquently because he was really upset. He put those words in a letter to some folk in a little Greek seaport in the middle of the first century AD. He had founded the community there around the teachings of Jesus of Nazareth, and now he had heard some bad news out of Corinth. Its members had forgotten all those values that had brought them together and were ripping each other apart. They had lost the love, you could say.

These Corinthians, Paul tells us, are fighting in the pews at church. They are splitting into factions according to who baptized them. People are suing each other. Sleeping with each other's spouses. The rich and high-status folk are demanding they get Communion first. Other people are getting drunk at Communion! This was some serious dysfunction. Amid all this, everybody's arguing about who is the better Christian, who is going to heaven and who is not.

This behavior sounds a little bit familiar. Tilt your head at it, and it sounds like a lot of us today on social media. Arrogant, rude, insisting on our own way, irritable, resentful, rejoicing in wrongdoing? Paul's got it, all right! It also sounds like some of our leaders in Washington, D.C. It sounds like some of our business leaders. It sounds like some of us in religious communities. It might even sound like heated conversations around the dinner table at Thanksgiving. The situation that occasioned the ancient epistle sounds remarkably contemporary.

Because we forgot: Love your neighbors! In our modern world, we lost this sense of love for our fellow humans. But for Paul and the disciples, love was something different. Love, to these Greeks, was a gift of the self to others. Love was rules for living.

Back in AD 50, Paul was furious. "Man," he says, basically, "I'm sure glad *I* didn't baptize any of you, because you make me sick." But he comes to them with an answer, offering the only corrective he sees for the mess they've gotten themselves into. The answer is love. Love isn't a sentiment—it's the only thing left to save a community divided.

You might think the opposite of love is hate. Watch

out—you're falling into the trap of vague sentiment again. If love looks outward, to the good of the other, then its opposite isn't hate. Its opposite is selfishness! It's a life completely centered on the self. Dr. King referred to this as the "reverse Copernican revolution."[1] To be selfish is to put yourself in the place of the sun, the whole universe revolving around you. Forget morality—at that point you've left reason behind. Life becomes a living lie. Because no amount of smarts, money, or accomplishments puts any one human at the center of existence.

Intuitively, we all understand that nothing good ever comes out of selfishness and greed. Selfishness is the most destructive force in all the cosmos, and hate is only its symptom. Selfishness destroys families. Selfishness destroys communities. Selfishness has destroyed societies, nations, and global communities, and it will destroy the human race by laying waste to our planet. If we let it.

Love Turns the World Upside Down

There's another problem when love becomes a mere sentiment. Love the sentiment—a nice feeling that rises up inside us—becomes love the sedative. It's a sweet thing that leaves us complacent and sleepy. No, the love I'm asking you to discover inside yourself, or reconnect to, is something fierce. This love is a verb: It's an action, with force and follow-through. When we pull love out of the abstract, really put it to work, it starts to reveal its extraordinary power.

Love as an action is the only thing that has ever changed the world for the better. Love is Martin Luther King, Mahatma Gandhi, and Josie Robbins. Love is a little girl in Pakistan named Malala Yousafzai standing up to armed men who said that girls shouldn't be educated. She was rescued and taken to England, where she could have retreated to a quiet life but instead made a commitment to spend her life working to improve other women's lives.

Love is Fannie Lou Hamer, whose contribution to the civil rights movement was honored on the floor of the U.S. House of Representatives in 2017, on the one hundredth anniversary of her birth. Fannie was one of twenty children. Her parents were two sharecroppers, de facto slaves. They were desperately poor. She had polio, but walking with a limp didn't stop her from picking cotton, so much cotton, in her teens. She dropped out of school to help her aging parents pick more cotton, because that's what a sister does when the family has nineteen other siblings to feed.

In 1961, she went to a Sunflower County hospital for a minor surgery and was sterilized without her consent. Some people would have given up at that point, deciding that any society that would condone such a crime was irrevocably evil. Not Fannie—she was just getting started. Because one year later, she learned something she hadn't heard before: Black people had the right to register and vote in the United States.* When she tried to do it in Ruleville, Mississippi, she failed the "literacy test," just one of the ways Whites have prevented Blacks from exercising their rights in our recent history. After that day, she never tired in her fight to right that wrong, surviving a KKK gunshot and the police beating her in prison. And despite the treatment she experienced at the hands of Whites, she never once backed down from the vision of the civil rights movement that had as its conclusion all good people living together as brothers and sisters, sharing the same welcoming table.

Love is equally the contribution of a woman like Frances Perkins, the secretary of labor who executed much of Roosevelt's New Deal. Perkins was born to a wealthy family. She could have gone to cotillion and then partied her life away. Instead, one day in 1911, when she was a young suffragette who had recently finished her master's in political science, she was walking in New York City's Washington Square Park with a friend when they heard screams. They followed the noise and saw men and women jumping out the windows of the Triangle Shirtwaist Factory, which was on fire. Ultimately 146 workers, most of them women, lost their lives in the blaze. Forever changed, Frances put her privilege to work. She dedicated

* At publication, whether to capitalize Black, White, and other races was being debated by editors and advocates across the United States. I chose to uppercase all the races referenced in this book, because it seemed most reflective of my beliefs: We honor everyone, equally. Consistent capitalization is also supported by the National Association of Black Journalists.

the rest of her life to lobbying to improve the lives of working people. She became the executive secretary for the Committee on Safety of the City of New York to fight for safer working conditions. Then she went to Washington. Because Frances Perkins loved America's workers, we now have minimum wage and overtime laws, and a forty-hour workweek. She also broke ground in the White House, as our first woman cabinet member.

Love's power isn't any less when it's one individual serving another. I was stunned when I read in 2018 about the informal network of Americans who came together spontaneously in the weeks after the Trump administration's adoption of a "zero tolerance" immigration policy that led to children being separated from their parents at the border. These citizens raised money so that more than a dozen women could be released from detention. They offered their homes so these women would have a safe place to sleep each night on their journeys of thousands of miles to their children in New York. They contributed cars and their time to drive them one leg of the trip, from home to home to home. They shared clothing, food, and care. And because these good Samaritans loved their neighbors, these women were finally reunited in New York City with the children who had been stolen from them. "Listen, this is our job," Immigrant Families Together founder Meghan Finn told the *New York Times*. "This is our job because our government did something really heinous to these families, and [getting them home] isn't just about putting them on a bus."

Love is a firefighter running into a burning building, risking his or her life for people he or she doesn't even know. Love is that first responder hurtling toward an emergency, a catastrophe, a disaster. Love is *someone* protesting anything that hurts or harms the children of God. Jesus said it this way, hours before his crucifixion: "No one has greater love than this, to lay down one's own life for one's friends."[2]

Love is a commitment to seek the good and to work for the good and welfare of others. It doesn't stop at our front door or our neighborhood, our religion or race, or our state's or your country's border. This is one great fellowship of love throughout the whole wide earth, as the hymn goes. It often calls us to step outside of what we thought our boundaries were, or what others expect of us. It calls for us to sacrifice, not because doing so feels good, but because it's the right thing to do.

Love as God's GPS for Living

Let's go back to Paul for a minute. After Paul reminds the AD 50 Facebookers what love looks like, he then comes out with these righteous words, which would fit nicely in a tweet: "And now faith, hope, and love abide . . . and the greatest of these is love."

Paul wasn't right about everything, not by far, but he was right about that. To live full lives, together, we need faith, hope, and love—but of these, love is the most important. *Faith* is another word for "trust." Without trust, society falls apart. Without trust, the world as we know it stops turning. Every economy—local, national, and global—depends on faith. A dollar bill is nothing but a piece of paper. Without trust, government is useless. Relationships are impossible. Without trust, it's every human for him- or herself—and that's a mess.

What about faith? Hans Küng, a Roman Catholic theologian, wrote that faith is a radical act of trust in reality. It is to dare to live and act as though the moral arc of the universe is long but bent toward justice, even if you can't see its end. Dare to live a life based on faith, and you're living a life that is often contrary to the easily observable evidence and to popular opinion. Faith is always in spite of.

The late senator Robert Kennedy, describing his own faith in the power of the good to overcome evil, would often quote the words of George Bernard Shaw: "Some men see things as they are and say, why; I dream things that never were and say, why not?"

Faith is William Wilberforce. I grew up in a home where his was a sacred and venerated name. My father went to Wilberforce University, an historically Black college in Ohio, founded by the African Methodist Episcopal (AME) Church and named after William. It was the first college to be owned and operated by African Americans; W.E.B. Du Bois had once been a professor there. It's also where my father and mother met, when he was in divinity school and she was teaching at the college.

Wilberforce was an eighteenth-century English evangelical for whom the gospel of Jesus of Nazareth was about both personal and social change. It was Wilberforce who introduced legislation in Parliament to end the slave trade. In 1779, when he first introduced the bill, he was shouted down and laughed at. He was ridiculed and ostracized from polite society. But he continued, year after year, from 1779 until 1807, when the tide of public opinion had changed and the slave trade came to a halt in the British Empire. And he continued the fight, until finally, in 1833, just a few days before his death, Parliament ended slavery, full stop, in the empire.

Nothing short of faith, in spite of the odds, can stay the course. Faith dares us to believe that in the end, love wins. We can't see it, but we believe it anyway.

Faith, with its partner *hope*, is why we pursue college degrees, follow passions, commit to the hard work of marriage and raising children. It's why we carry protest signs and campaign for candidates, instead of just sitting around watching *America's Got Talent*. (I say that as someone who counts *America's Got Talent* as one of my favorite television shows.)

Then hope comes along, and puts wind in our sails of faith. Hope is the energy that keeps us going when the gravity of reality would otherwise defeat us. It was Dante who pictured the words "Abandon hope all who enter here" over the gates of hell. Without hope, life become mere existence and survival. But with hope, you can "march through hell for a heavenly cause" if you have to. But while faith and hope are necessary for a full life, they're not a *guide* for life. They don't tell you what to do. That's love's job. Love tells you how to direct the energy of outrageous faith. If hope and faith are the wind and sails, love is the rudder. It's God's GPS.

When I was interviewed for the *Harvard Business Review*, the interviewer said, "Love's great, but how does it apply to a CEO?" Because we've forgotten agape, we think love is removed from business. Actually, it's as simple— and I'll admit, as difficult—for a CEO as it is for anyone. To switch on God's GPS, simply ask yourself a question: Is this just about *me,* or is it about *we*? Does this decision serve only my unenlightened self-interest, or does it somehow serve the greater good? And if the answer is *me, me, me, and only me,* you don't do it. It's that simple. Me or we?

The problem with a *me* approach to life is that if it's only or primarily about me, there is no or little room for *you*. And if everyone thinks, lives, and acts that way, there will be no room for any of us. What the late congresswoman Shirley Chisholm often said of the American experiment in democracy is true for us as a global human community: "We came over here on different ships, but we're all in the same boat now."

John Donne, the sixteenth-century priest and poet, said it this way: "Any man's death diminishes me, because I am involved in mankind, and therefore never send to know for whom the bell tolls; it tolls for thee."

In his "Letter from a Birmingham Jail," Dr. King said it this way: "We are caught in an inescapable network of mutuality, tied in a single garment of destiny. Whatever affects one directly, affects all indirectly."

Archbishop Desmond Tutu said it this way: "I am because we are," which is the central principle of Ubuntu, the oral tradition of wisdom in southern African traditional cultures.

And that's what St. Paul was getting at. That's what love is about. Where selfishness excludes, love makes room and includes. Where selfishness puts down, love lifts up. Where selfishness hurts and harms, love helps and heals. Where selfishness enslaves, love sets free and liberates.

The way of love will show us the right thing to do, every single time. It is moral and spiritual grounding—and a place of rest—amid the chaos that is often part of life. It's how we stay decent in indecent times. Loving is not always easy, but like with muscles, we get stronger both with repetition and as the burden gets heavier. And it works.

CHAPTER 2

Looking for God

Question: How do I find God's love?

> *Where true love is found, God himself is there.*
> —"UBI CARITAS," MEDIEVAL HYMN

SOMETIMES IT'S HARD to feel God's love in our every-day lives, especially when chaos descends. We all have responsibilities and mundane routines. Maybe you've heard the saying that a marriage is no more than two people asking each other every night, "What's for dinner?" Sometimes life itself feels that way. We also have challenges and frustrations, from aching feet to unpaid bills to broken relationships. We have old injuries, and open wounds, and fears about the future—all those terrifying possibilities we can't control.

No, we can't always feel transcendent. We don't always have a chorus of angels in our ear. But there is good news. There is a simple way to connect to the divine, anytime you feel like it. If God is love, and love is an action, you've only got to get out there and *do* it. You've got to get out there and *receive* it. And the easiest way to do that is to become part of a community of people who want to give and receive love, to liberate themselves from the tyranny of self to look outward. From a small gesture to a large sacrifice, every day provides an opportunity to do love, so long as you're not living a life in isolation. And if you've got a loving community, you can rest in God's hands anytime you need to.

Community has been my conduit to the safe harbor of God's love my whole life, but especially since I was ten years old. Until then, my life had been quiet and secure in our little East Buffalo community. But that summer, everything changed.

My family had driven down from Buffalo to visit my maternal grandmother in her apartment in Yonkers, New York. We all spent the day at Playland, an amusement park with roller coasters, a beach, and a boardwalk. My sister, my cousins, and I had the time of our lives. We came home happy and worn out. I don't remember much else, until the middle of the night. We kids were bunking in the living room, and noises and flashing lights outside woke me up. I peeked out of my sleeping bag and saw lights on in the dining room. Paramedics came through with their red equipment bags. I wasn't scared exactly, but I was confused. What was going on?

When everyone left, Grandma sat down with us on the couch. Mommy was sick, she said. They had taken her to the hospital to check her out. Daddy was with her.

Grandma was calm and matter-of-fact. She probably didn't have enough information yet to know how bad things were, but I'm sure she must've been scared inside. Her daughter, Dorothy, had been taken away in the middle of the night in an ambulance.

The next morning our father came home and told us Mommy's brain—her brilliant mathematician's brain—had been bleeding. She had gone into a coma. He explained that meant she was sleeping, and we didn't know yet when she'd wake up. We couldn't visit her, he said, because children weren't allowed in the hospital. (That was customary back then.)

The adults did a good job at making it seem like everything would be OK, somehow. So we kids stayed busy with our bikes and board games, letting the grown-ups do the worrying for us. After some days or weeks—in my child's memory, I only know that it seemed like a very long time—Daddy drove us back to Buffalo. Mommy stayed in the hospital, Mount Sinai, because she wasn't stable enough to be moved. It felt strange and sad to be leaving without her.

At that point began what must have been one of the hardest periods of my father's life. When I look back, I say to myself, "*God almighty, how did he do it?*" Daddy would lead Sunday services at St. Philip's in Buffalo, then take off for the eight-hour drive to New York to be with my mother. On Thursday, he'd drive the eight hours back and go straight back to work—leading Bible study, praying with folk, keeping the church's many programs running, alongside all the administrative and organizing work that falls to a parish priest.

We were a close-knit family. Now my mother had been taken from us in the middle of the night, and my father was gone half the week to care for her. This period could have made an indelible and traumatic mark on me. It could have planted in me the feeling—not that I would have been able to articulate it yet—that the world was a cruel and random place. That love was as fragile and fleeting as our human bodies. I could have lost my childhood.

But that's not what happened. My cousin Bill was from Ohio and had recently graduated from Kent State. He was in the market for a teaching job, and instead of staying in Ohio, he decided he would search for it in Buffalo so that he could help us out. He ended up working for the Buffalo Public Schools until his retirement, which is to say that the fundamental geography of his life was shaped by his willingness to be there when family needed him.

Meanwhile, the community rose up around us. These were people from my father's church, and they all lived in roughly the same neighborhood of East Buffalo—the Black neighborhood, formerly the Polish neighborhood, which all sat east of Main Street. (Today the neighborhood no longer exists because of urban renewal, which some folks used to call "Negro removal." The Kensington Expressway, completed in 1971, would ultimately chop the neighborhood in two.) Our church was roughly half

West Indian and half American Black, from a variety of backgrounds. Because Buffalo was segregated by race more than by class, doctors and white-collar workers lived alongside a larger majority of working-class people. There were domestic workers and janitors, cooks and servers. Plenty of people were struggling, or something close to it. But that didn't stop them from extending a hand, or even their wallet, when someone needed it. They were opinionated, politically engaged people, always debating or fussing about something.

Sometimes my grandma would drive back up with my father to stay with us. But when she couldn't, we spent Sunday night to Thursday morning at Dr. and Mrs. Bullock's house. Dr. Bullock was a dentist. We liked going there because they had the sweetest dog, Mr. K, and a cat, too. Sometimes we brought our own cats, Furry and Hercules, and it became a real menagerie.

Another lady, Erna Clark, the Sunday-school superintendent, picked us up and took us to school every day. She worked in a government office nearby. I already told you about Josie Robbins, who took us on all those outings. These folks weren't just loving on us; they were on top of our every move. They were *tough*. Mrs. Bullock would check my homework at night, and Ms. Clark would ask me about it again in the morning. Years later, Ms. Clark would suggest I take a look at Hobart and William Smith Colleges, where I ultimately went and which I otherwise wouldn't have known existed.

After many months of this routine, we finally got news that Mommy could be moved to a nursing home in Buffalo for long-term care. She would be back in time for Christmas. That was the only Christmas of my childhood that I didn't care about toys. All we could think about was our mother coming back.

If I was nervous about seeing her again, I don't remember it. I just wanted to be in the same room as her, to hold her hand. When we all filed into her room at the nursing home, she was on her back in bed, with a white feeding tube in her nose. Her eyes were closed, and she could breathe independently. My beautiful mother.

Every night after dinner, we went to see her. Daddy told us not to whisper but to speak just as though she were awake, in case she could hear. We sat and talked to her, watched TV, said prayers, and kissed her good night, night after night. We didn't know whether she was conscious of any of it, but sometimes it felt like she had moments. She might tighten her grip while she was holding your hand. Sometimes she'd even open her eyes, and it felt like she was seeing you. But she never spoke again. This lasted for several years.

MY PARENTS MET and fell in love when my mother was teaching college math at Wilberforce, where my father was in seminary. He had come from a long line of Baptist preachers. For her undergrad, my mother had gone to

West Virginia State, at that time a Black college, then received her master's in mathematics from the University of Chicago. Keep in mind, this was the 1940s. For a woman, and a Black woman at that, to study math at the University of Chicago, she must've been pretty special.

It was because of my mother that my father became an Episcopal priest. They had both been raised Baptist, but she had become an Episcopalian in Chicago. While they were dating, she took my father to church. They were among the few Black parishioners in the pews that day. My father was amazed, but dubious, when it came time for Communion. The priest welcomed everyone to receive the body and blood of Christ—and from a single communal chalice! Again, this was the 1940s. Jim Crow was alive and well. It was the North, but segregation and separation of the races was still the law of the land. President Franklin Roosevelt had just a few years earlier issued an executive order desegregating defense industries. The armed forces had not yet been integrated. *Brown v. the Board of Education of Topeka* had not yet happened. The Montgomery bus boycott had not yet happened. Martin Luther King was still in seminary. And my father saw one cup from which everyone was to drink. One cup! One cup?

My father hung back, as my mother went forward. He wondered if the priest would really offer her the common cup. And if he did, would others continue to drink from the same cup? He held his breath as my mother sipped.

And as the cup was passed, the next person did drink. And the next. And the next. And the next. When he told that story, he would always say, *"Any church in which Blacks and Whites drink out of the same cup knows something about the Gospel that I want to be a part of."* And so my mother led my father down a path that he probably would never have taken for himself—love in action.

My mother used to call me *Michaelovich*—why, I don't know, but I loved it, her pet name for me. One day at our house in Buffalo, I was playing on the couch and somehow managed to get my head stuck in it. I was probably five years old. I started hollering in panic, sure that my situation was irreversible. My mom rushed to the scene and easily managed to disentangle me. Then she drew me into her chest. *Michaelovich, Michaelovich*, she whispered. Years later I could still hear her voice saying that name in my head. We sat there rocking on the couch, how long I don't know. Long enough that my shaking body relaxed and settled.

MY MOTHER NEVER did wake up from her coma. For years, we visited, and hoped. But eventually her body shut itself down. My memory of her death is vague. What I do remember vividly is the cemetery. I think it must have been the moment when I finally understood that Mommy wasn't coming back.

The day we buried her, it was frigid even for a Buffalo

winter. We were used to the cold, but that day it seemed colder. It was a cold that wanted to crush you. That's Buffalo's winter, but that's also just death, a cold, low-life, horrible thing. "Jordan's river is chilly and cold. Chill my body but not my soul," goes the spiritual. As they lowered her body into the ground, I started crying. I was standing next to Mrs. Bullock, and she pulled me into her. "Mommy's gone," I told her. "It's so cold." Mrs. Bullock rocked and rocked me. I felt the soft, scratchy hairs of her wool coat on my cheek and rubbed against them. Solid. We rocked and rocked.

That memory is a moment, and more than a moment. The way Mrs. Bullock pulled me in, her coat a soft landing for a boy's suffering—this is how we lived through the whole time of Mommy's sickness and her death. We were always resting in the loving hands of our church community. Which is to say, in God's hands.

Grandma, a Baptist, never understood the quiet, orderly Episcopalians in my father's parish on Sunday. She used to call us "woo-woo" Martians, silent and shuffling around the church. "How do you know when the Holy Spirit comes in your church?" she would rib my daddy, both of them laughing. "Nobody gets the spirit and gets up and shouts! If it ain't in the prayer book, you don't say it!" She much preferred the joy of Sundays at the Baptist church.

After Mommy's burial, we gathered at someone's house

for a meal. My grandmother looked around the room at the Bullocks, Josie Robbins, and all the rest. She shook her head and caught my eye. "You know where the spirit of the Lord is," she said to me, "when you see people love." She shook her head and smiled.

Grandma had no idea she was echoing the medieval hymn "Ubi Caritas": "Where true love is found, God himself is there." She had come by her wisdom the honest way—from a life of hardship and loving. She knew the Bible says, "God is love." And she knew that the power of that love is often mediated through the people who love us. And it's those people and that love that pull us through and keep us going when we don't have the strength.

Remember St. Paul? "Love never ends." My mother was gone. But love wasn't. Human beings—fragile as we are—are the beautiful, heartbreaking conduit, but ultimately not the source. I didn't have these thoughts at ten years old, but I could feel it. I knew that I was loved as much as ever, as well as ever, and that though I missed my mother, we would make it.

That doesn't mean that losing someone is easy. Grief is real, and travels to your core. Even now I find myself hoping to recall her voice—*Michaelovich*—in my mind. Holidays like Christmas, especially when I was a child, were different without her. Everything was different without her. She wasn't there at birthdays, graduations, weddings. She wasn't there to see grandchildren. I suppose over time the loss becomes manageable, but it never completely goes away.

Understanding that love never ends does not erase grief. The prayer book introduces the liturgy of the dead by reminding us that even Jesus wept at his friend's grave. Joy and grief coexist. As well, that love that the New Testament says "never ends" is also described in the Hebrew as "strong as death." I've begun to see how that is true; we will always grieve those we love when they are no longer living. And yet, the love we humans experience, as powerful and durable as it is, is only a faint reflection of God's love, which is eternal, the source of all love and loves. And that is the love that welcomes and embraces those we love when this mortal life is over.

While I haven't actually seen a copy of the bulletin from my mother's funeral, this passage from the writings of St. Paul in Romans 8 was probably read. It was a favorite of my father's, who would have selected the readings for the service.

Who will separate us from the love of Christ? Will hardship, or distress, or persecution, or famine, or nakedness, or peril, or sword? As it is written, "For your sake we are being killed all day long; we are accounted as sheep to be slaughtered."

No, in all these things we are more than conquerors through him who loved us. For I am convinced that neither death, nor life, nor angels, nor rulers, nor things present, nor things to come, nor powers, nor height, nor depth, nor anything else in all creation, will be able to separate us from the love of God in Christ Jesus our Lord.

The love of God does not end. And if that is so, neither does life. And so *The Book of Common Prayer* says that in death, "life is changed, not ended."

Finding Rituals of Comfort

God may be the source of love, but people are often the vessels. Once you understand that, you also start to understand that connecting to the Holy Spirit isn't about what we say in our house of worship on a Sunday. It's not even whether we're *in* church on a Sunday. It's the community of love we create for ourselves and for others. When that happens, God's there. That's God showing up. We're resting in God's hands.

Faith communities, I'd add, have hands to rest in that are especially strong. They have been the custodians to a particularly well-established tool kit, honed by centuries, for those times when life—let's be honest—*sucks*, like when loved ones pass. I'm talking about rituals and traditions, and supports to lean on when we're lost and bereft, or trying to help someone who is. Rituals move us forward through grief. They're another means of resting in God's hands.

I got this, viscerally, many years after my mother's

death, at the first funeral I led as the pastor of St. James Episcopal Church in Baltimore, when I was a young priest in my late thirties and mid-forties. The man going into the ground that day was just a kid, maybe nineteen years old. His name was Dwayne. He was caught up in the gang world, gunned down on the sidewalk by a rival. Dwayne's mother had been a parishioner way back. That day, as I looked into the crowd, the congregation felt noticeably different. Church regulars were there, but many pews were occupied by his young circle of friends. There were at least a hundred. I didn't know any of them personally, because we hadn't yet started the community outreach that became our focal point in later years. Looking out, I was hit by a realization: We've got a whole generation of kids who are now growing into adulthood, whose only rituals and commandments are those of the streets.

As I watched them fumble through the service, I tried to change things up to meet them where they were. They were grieving, and the last thing I wanted was for them to leave feeling alienated. During the sermon, I spoke to them directly, about grief, but also about hope. When it came time for Communion, I explained the tradition of bread and wine in remembrance of Christ's sacrifice, and many came up to receive it.

At the cemetery, several of Dwayne's friends served as pallbearers. No one should have to teach a bunch of twenty-year-olds how to hoist their friend inside a box, but the funeral director gently issued instructions. Together they carried their friend's coffin to the gravesite, where family covered it with flowers. When the prayers were finished, the funeral director invited everyone for a repast back at the church.

At that point, people typically greet the family, then trickle back to their cars. But the pallbearers didn't move from the coffin. One of them put his hand on it and said, "Dwayne, we'll see you real soon."

We'll see you real soon.

I watched in silence as they rested their hands on the coffin, and stood there, not sure where to go next.

Real soon, Dwayne.

For these kids, death, not love, was God. They had a community, but it didn't look anything like Jesus. Remember that Curtis Mayfield song "If there's a Hell below, we're all going to go, go, go, go, go"? If death is your god, life is a nightmare. These guys loved their brothers, but in some sense it was perverted, because they had lost faith in anything but death. The rituals they did observe were far from what some call the habits of grace. These were rituals of destruction.

We'll see you real soon, Dwayne.

Ritual, prayer, and meditation, traditionally guided by religious communities, have been around for a long time. They've had the beta testing of centuries of practitioners. These practices allow us to navigate those times when words are inadequate. They help us take care of ourselves and others in a way that doesn't feel cheap or reductive.

While my mother was sick, my family never stopped living the rituals of faith, whether they felt like it or not. My father never missed a church service, and that was more than it being his job. I think that's why we prayed good and long each time we visited Mommy—we didn't know what else to do. These words—*oh, help us, heavenly father*—carried us when we couldn't carry ourselves. We rested in God's hands.

The late senator John McCain spoke about how prayer got him through imprisonment in Vietnam. As a kid, he had gone to Episcopal High School in Alexandria, Virginia. The priests led the kids through morning prayers every single day. He said the prayers then because he had to. And yet, when he was stuck in that cell, staring at four walls, with no way of knowing what misery the days and weeks and months ahead held, he started every day with prayer. It kept him going. He rested in God's hands.

In the Bible, after the Crucifixion, Mary Magdalene weeps, hollers, and screams. Christ had saved her from demons, and now he was dead. Then she stops screaming and gets busy. She wasn't feeling any better, no. But she had a job to do. She had to go to Christ's tomb to carry out the rituals of faith. So she went. She prepared the oil, then she was set to anoint the body, and what happened? She stumbled headlong into the miracle of the resurrection. I swear to you she did not see that coming! If she hadn't been going through the motions, she would have missed the miracle! She'd be home in bed, depressed and senseless. Instead, she rested in God's hands and witnessed the impossible.

Even Jesus himself knew to rest in God's hands! In the Protestant tradition, there was a time when Good Friday services centered on his last seven words on the cross. They pulled the final words from all the gospels and put them together. In Luke's Gospel, the last thing Jesus says is, "Father, into your hands I commend my spirit." Jesus is actually quoting Psalm 31. It's not an accident that several of his final words are, in fact, quotes from the Psalms. The Psalms would have been familiar hymns or chants that he would have heard his whole life. These were the words that might be sung by a mother to her child. In his dying moments, in agony, he leans on the spiritual tradition that nurtured him. Those words bubble up and carry him through. He rested in God's hands.

Community is love, and intentional spiritual practices provide the scaffolding that makes it even stronger. And so at fourteen years old, I did not conclude that the world was a broken, bitter, and ruthless place. I was not abandoned—I was loved.

And if I wasn't abandoned, neither was my mother. She was also resting in God's hands. None of us know how it all works out. We don't know everything. But this we do know: *Father, into your hands I commend my spirit.* There was a hymn in the old Episcopal hymnal:

O Love that wilt not let me go,
I rest my weary soul in thee;
I give thee back the life I owe,
That in thine ocean depths its flow
May richer, fuller be.

I came to believe that's what heaven's about. Our loved ones go to rest in the pure love that we see only intimations of in life.

When I was an adult, my extended community unexpectedly brought Mommy back to me—not once, but twice. The first time was during my years as the pastor of St. Simon's, in Lincoln Heights, Ohio. A mile down the road from the church sat the convent of the Sisters of Transfiguration, who you'll hear more about later. The nuns there took care of a woman named Grace. Grace had a disease that had left her face and body severely disfigured and in need of special ongoing medical attention. Her face was covered in tumors, to the extent that they twisted up her mouth, making it difficult for her to drink, eat, and speak normally.

Grace's job at the convent was to sit in the lobby, welcoming visitors and helping them get wherever they were going. One day, my godmother, Sister Althea Augustine, who was one of the sisters, told me that Grace wanted to speak with me. I found her at the desk where she sat in the vestibule of the convent, and she led me to one of the little side rooms, where we sat on the couch. I had spoken with Grace only casually and had no idea what she wanted to get off her chest.

Grace told me she had once lived in a church-run home in Chicago that was for people with incurable diseases. Many of the residents were housebound and dealing with the loneliness and real isolation that comes with being so sick you can't live a normal life. To cheer them up, a group of women from the church came to visit on a regular basis. They'd sit and talk, offering fellowship and a glimpse of normalcy.

"Your mother was in that group," Grace told me. "I remember she was in grad school at the time, and she loved to talk to me about C. S. Lewis." She told me my mother had caught the Lewis bug thanks to his book *Mere Christianity*. I had assumed, or maybe my father had told me, that my godmother, Althea, had turned my mother on to the Episcopal faith. But here, suddenly, was new information. Of course Lewis would appeal to my mother, the logical, rational mathematician. It made sense. It was like my mother had been spirited back to give me a fuller picture of her truth. I was blown away. I could no longer see any disfigurement in the woman who sat across from me. It was like she was pure, embodied spirit—which is exactly what people are, embodied spirits. We just can't always see it.

"She was just lovely," Grace told me. Then she took my hands. "Ever since you came here, when you give me Communion, I've been thinking to myself, '*He has his mother's hands.*' I thought you might want to know that." More than thirty years after my mother's death, Grace gave me a new experience of her. I was resting in God's hands again that day.

More recently, I was in Northern California to ordain a new bishop. While there, I led a conversation with the diocese's clergy about how to live Jesus's teachings in our personal lives and in the public square. Afterward, we went next door to break for lunch. The dean of the cathedral stopped me on the way. "I'd like to introduce you to someone," he said, walking me toward an African American woman with glasses, a seashell necklace, and gold hoop earrings. He introduced her as Margaret, and we greeted each other with a hug. She seemed barely older than me, but turned out to be ninety-three years young. Margaret smiled broadly before pressing a four-by-six-inch card into my hand. I looked at it curiously. There was a line drawing of a large nineteenth-century-style mansion and fir trees, all covered in snow. Still more curious, I turned it over and saw that it was a postcard. Above the cursive greeting— "Hi old lady"—was the printed location: MacCorkle Hall, West Virginia State College. My mother's school. The postcard was signed, "Dorothy Strayhorne." My mother.

My mother, Margaret told me, had been her roommate. "I've been trying to catch up on work, since I've been loafing," the postcard read. (My mother, loafing!) We sat down together for lunch, and Margaret caught me up on that period of my mother's life. She had the final missing piece of the story of how my mother (and therefore I) had ended up Episcopalian. Margaret was a Quaker from New Jersey, but there had been no Quaker meeting-house on or near campus. My mother agreed to try the Episcopal church with her, and that's where it all began. She told me that my mother had gone to the University of Chicago with a scholarship from the Rosenwald Fund, which was founded by one of the owners of Sears, Roebuck and Company to improve educational opportunities for Blacks in the rural South. She could remember my mother pledging Alpha Kappa Alpha, the oldest Greek sorority for Black women. I told her that my daughter had followed in her footsteps at AKA, in honor of the grandmother she never knew.

As we were finishing lunch, Margaret looked at me and said, "You know, you look so much like her." Love never dies, and there I was, resting in God's hands again.

RESTING IN GOD's hands, building a community of love, is more than going to a house of worship, or any place community gathers. To journey to "resting" is actually active—you have to be willing to ask for help, and to receive it when it's offered. No easy feat. But it's a lot easier to do when your community shares a desire to live in the spirit of agape.

"Join a faith community" seems like an easy answer. But that's really not the case. You can go there, but you still got to *do* love. You put yourself out there, with all the vulnerability that requires. You need help and you ask for it. When someone asks you for help, you give it freely. You don't have to be in a faith community to do those things—but it takes a lot more bravery to do it anywhere, anytime. When you ask for help in a church, mosque, or temple, you pretty much know you're going to get an "amen."

Others might find their comfort in a deeper truth: Love is all around us. It is in nature—in the ocean, the trees, the sky, the mountains, all of it. But connecting to God's presence in nature isn't passive, either. It requires active presence.

The great theologian and philosopher Howard Thurman, who wrote a book on mysticism, among other subjects, had an early brush with the divine when he watched Halley's comet. Thurman was looking up at a sky few of us can imagine; it was 1910 and there were no lights in his town to dim the heavens. He and his mother watched the comet fill the darkness with light as it made its journey across the sky.

Thurman felt terror for a moment—after all, for weeks everyone had been talking about the possibly terrible aftermath of the comet falling from the sky. But his mother was calm, reassuring him that God would keep them safe. Something shifted in Thurman, and the fear left him. He felt one with the comet, and a sudden awareness and awe of what created and controlled the comet. In reflection, Thurman gave a name to this awareness, "the givenness of God," which the human heart by its very nature hungers to connect with. When we succeed, we feel it: *He's got the whole world in his hands.*

I'll leave you with the hymn "His Eye Is on the Sparrow," made famous today by the singer Lauryn Hill. "I sing because I'm happy, I sing because I'm free, for His eye is on the sparrow, and I know He watches me." God's love is everywhere, in all things, and that includes you.

CHAPTER 3

Making Do and Making New

Question: How do I find the energy to keep loving when the world seems to be going the other way?

*I have been in Sorrow's kitchen and licked out all the pots.
Then I have stood on the peaky mountain wrapped in
rainbows with a harp and a sword in my hands.*
—Zora Neale Hurston, *Dust Tracks on a Road*

MY ELDERS, AND so many folk like them, lived hard lives, much harder than I've had to—and yet they discerned, divined, or discovered some secrets to life and real joy amid unthinkable sorrow, hardship, and heartache.

The Harlem Renaissance writer Zora Neale Hurston deftly captured this miraculous mixture of hardship and hope. I remember hearing my elders put their own spin on it, adding the word "clean" with emphasis: "I've been in Sorrow's kitchen and licked all the pots—*clean.*" That's how bad it was.

These were the same folk from whom I learned much about living a life defined and directed by the way of love.

These were the folk who lived by the motto "Never let anyone drag you so low as to hate them." These were folk who figured out how to harness the energy of love when everything about life seems to be draining that energy away. They licked the pot in Sorrow's kitchen clean. But they also stood on the mountaintop wrapped in a rainbow with a sword of victory in the midst of the struggle in their hands. So how did they do it?

FOR ME, the answer begins in my grandmother's kitchen. I sat so many times at the Formica table, watching my grandma work, talking to her, listening to her, eating. In the eye of my mind and heart I can see her there now. Her favorite apron like a uniform that had been worn in many a battle, slipping off one shoulder. Gray hair pulled into a neat bun. She's rinsing the greens, dumping the grit. Chopping and chopping. She's snapping the peas and, near New Year's, rinsing the chitterlings. (If the truth be told, at least in those days, if someone was cleaning chitterlings, you didn't hang around too long.) While she worked, whatever she was cooking or baking or prepping, she told us stories.

One of the realities of our life growing up in Buffalo, and that of many like us, was that while we lived in the North, we were rooted in the South. You could say we were in exile, from old Jim Crow and the reign of terror all the way back to the end of Reconstruction. Like other peoples who migrate, immigrate, or live in diaspora from their native home, urban Blacks with Southern roots brought home with them.

That meant that though we lived North, we ate South. Grits, collards, fried everything you can imagine, hot sauces, well-spiced food, desserts galore, sweet tea, and on and on. Open the bathroom cupboard and you'd find every hair-care product Madam C. J. Walker invented. News from the African American diaspora in America was readily available through *Jet* or *Ebony* magazines; the Black newspapers in Buffalo at the time, *The Challenger* and *The Criterion*; and the radio stations WUFO-AM and WBLK-FM. We were connected and interconnected with home, which was south of the Mason-Dixon Line, and ultimately across the Atlantic.

South came north and Africa traversed the Atlantic. Grandma, whose home was in eastern North Carolina, in towns like Winton, Murfreesboro, and Ahoskie, is the icon of all that for me.

NELLIE GOLDIE ROYSTER STRAYHORNE was not unlike many others of her time. She was African American, the daughter of sharecroppers, granddaughter of former slaves. Family lore had it that she had some Indian in her, evidenced by high cheekbones and hair that showed periodic evidence of being straight, without a hot comb making it that way. That wasn't an uncommon claim among Black folk in those days. Oral tradition had it that Native Americans befriended runaway slaves when they could.

She went to high school and later taught young children in the old country segregated schools. She worked as a domestic, cleaning homes, while rearing children and a family. She never went to college, but she made sure her children did. She buried some of her own children, one of whom was our mother. She buried a husband and lost loved ones fighting for this country, in segregated units, during the Second World War.

I watched her as she stood cleaning greens, pounds and pounds of them, getting ready to work one of her culinary miracles. She was there most often around the time my mother died, when I was a preteen. I still had the hands of a boy, my body all awkward angles, hair unsuccessfully styled in the popular 'do of the time, *the wave*. I didn't realize then that she was serving more than food when she heaped the collards, rice and gravy, and fried chicken or pork chops or fish onto your plate. All I knew then was it was delicious, especially if you could get to the leftovers first the next day and run off with some cold fried chicken. That's when it tasted the best. It may not have always been good for you, but it was sure good to the taste, and what it represented was good for the soul. The food was just plain good.

I realize that now, because while she was prepping and cooking, she would tell stories. My sister and I, and sometimes our cousin Ronald, would sit around and listen. I wish I had recorded them. Some were her childhood stories of growing up sharecropping. Her father worked the land. Their landowner was apparently kind and benevolent, as they went. Grandma's family didn't have a lot. Times were hard and sometimes dangerous. But they always "made do" with what they had and what life threw at them. That was the phrase she would use. "We made do."

If Grandma's cooking was "making do," then we know what "making do" really means. It means taking grits and making them gourmet. It means creating a meal for your family that tastes like love feels. A meal so delicious you forget your troubles, at least while you're at the table.

The food Grandma was cooking, which was our normal diet, was what the writer Amiri Baraka would in a few years rightly dub *soul food*. It was a wonderful fusion of West African foods and flavors and Southern habits—and an act of incredible practical creativity. In his book *Soul Food: The Surprising Story of an American Cuisine, One Plate at a Time,* Professor Adrian Miller writes that soul food was specifically the food cooked by Black migrants to the north, who came poor and stayed poor. "Black cooks had no choice but to continue to stretch most meals by using cheap cuts of meat and lots of inexpensive vegetables and starches—foods that class-conscious whites rejected or ate when no one was watching."[1]

Going back further, the food has origins in the limited foods that were rations for slaves. They weren't given a lot, and they weren't given the best cuts. They were given what was often not wanted, scraps otherwise thrown away. Part of the genius of soul food way back to its origins was that folk figured out how to "make it stretch." They took the proverbial two pieces of fish and five loaves of bread and fed a multitude. For the slaves, "stretching it" was part sharing, part culinary skill.

But the other part of the miracle was the taste. The flavoring of West Africa and Native American herbs and vegetables, along with the innards and inconceivable parts from virtually every part of the pig, created food that tasted so good that the quality overcame the need for excessive quantity. Your palate was satisfied with less. It all borders on the miraculous.

A friend of mine, Bishop Clifton "Danny" Daniels, who was the bishop of the Eastern Episcopal Diocese in North Carolina when I served in the central one, told me about one of his clergy who had moved to California and later returned. She knew she was back in the South, he said, when she could go to the butcher shop and find all the parts you needed to reconstitute the entire pig.

My ancestors took a little and made a lot. They took what was left over and made sure no one was left out. They took foods that were put down and cast out by others and lifted the hungry up. That's a miracle. That's taking what is old and making something new. That's making do!

But there is an important caveat: Making do is not the same as giving up or giving in to the status quo. It's a way of figuring out how to both survive and thrive. Making do is like the potter and the clay in the Bible. The Bible describes this way of engaging life and existence as nothing less than the creative work of God expressed in humanity:

> Yet, O Lord, you are our Father;
> we are the clay, and you are our potter;
> we are all the work of your hand.[2]

Making do is about molding and making, taking what is old, what is given, what is, and making something new. It's about taking an old reality and creating a new possibility. Making garbage gourmet.

In the New Testament there is a passage in which the Apostle Paul reflects on living the logic of love. It begins with the words "Let love be genuine; hate what is evil, hold fast to what is good." Then it concludes with, "Do not be overcome by evil, but overcome evil with good."[3]

That is the methodology, the way, the logic of love. Soul food follows the same supernatural logic. Overcome evil with good. Take their garbage and serve it back gourmet. That is the way of love that Jesus was getting at, over and over. That's making do.

The Recipe for Making Do

I know, that all sounds good. But how do you do it? How do you turn the problem of reality into possibility? Grandma's kitchen may help again, but allow me to talk you into it with the help of one of my favorite poems, Elizabeth Barrett Browning's "Aurora Leigh."

The poem reflects on the story of Moses. Moses started out as a fairly self-absorbed guy and somehow ended up the sacrificial leader who delivered the Hebrew slaves to freedom. His moment of transformation happened one day when he was tending sheep on the hillside of a volcano. He saw a light, maybe fire, up the way, so he went to investigate. As he got closer, he realized it was a bush that seemed to be burning and yet was not consumed.

Then he heard the voice of God telling him to take off his shoes, because the ground under his feet was holy. Moses did it, and what do you know, God struck up a conversation. And because of that conversation, Moses went down the mountain and led the campaign of plagues (the ancient equivalent of a boycott) and negotiations, and eventually liberated the Hebrew slaves from Egypt.

That's the story Elizabeth Barrett Browning was riffing on when she wrote this:

> Earth's crammed with heaven,
> And every common bush afire with God;
> But only he who sees, takes off his shoes;
> The rest sit round it and pluck blackberries.

A grandmother at work in the kitchen is—or once upon a time, was—quite common and ordinary. But sometimes the *extra* is hidden right there in the ordinary. So forgive me, but let me take off my shoes as I remember that kitchen.

There were at least three things helping Grandma out in that kitchen that I can see: tradition, imagination, and God.

Ingredient One: Tradition

Think about tradition for a second. I don't mean a dusty old attic filled with stuff from the past. I mean tapping the time-tested wisdom of ancestors, a spiritual lineage of wisdom for living. Grandma and all real cooks don't create from nothing. She learned something about cooking from her elders. And they from theirs. She wasn't re-inventing the wheel, so to speak. She was building on culinary traditions, skills honed and perfected by trial and error over time. When she was cooking and thinking and making choices about how much of this and that, she was building on a long wisdom tradition about how to feed folk and make them want to eat.

Beyond food, she and others like her were steeped in an old oral tradition of wisdom. Aunt Lillian, grandma's sister, would say to us kids before we went to school, "You go get your learning, because once it's in your head, nobody can take that away." Or she'd say, "What the Lord gave, only the Lord can take." I never asked where they got all those expressions, and if I had, I don't think they could have said. It was just in the water, and I know from comparing notes with other Black kids who grew up at the same time that they were hearing it, too.

Now I see that these casual sayings were drawn from a deep well of wisdom, one passed down from my grandmother's ancestors. No one knew better how to rise up in defiant joy than Negro slaves. They gave us soul food, and they gave us the mother wit baked within it. When we look for guidance on how to live a life grounded in and guided by the way of love, we don't need to start from scratch when there is wisdom from people of faith who have struggled and yet made do.

Religion at its best is not an old cobweb-filled attic called tradition, and it's not "the way we've always done it." It's a treasure chest of wisdom gleaned from human beings who have dared, as the Bible says of someone called Enoch, to walk with God.

Just like Grandma cooking in the kitchen, we don't have to start from scratch. We can build on some time-tested paths to spirituality and faith that have worked in the past and that can evolve for the realities of today.

Ingredient Two: Imagination

Michelangelo, certainly one of the greatest artists who ever lived, said that a sculpture was already complete in a block of granite before he picked up his chisel. But it was his job, the sculptor's job, to discover it. That's imagination!

Grandma saw the same potential in raw, unprocessed ingredients. Vegetables, ordinary poultry, meats, and fish could be chiseled into something tasty and wonderful.

Long ago, Aristotle pointed out the grand truth that a simple acorn already holds the potential of a gigantic oak tree. On some level, Grandma, and cooks all over the world, knew how to do the creative work to get the acorn to become the oak tree.

Somebody else once said that problems are solutions in disguise. While that may be overly simplified, I think Grandma got that, too. She was an expert at what psychologists today might call "reframing." I remember one day getting a peach out of the refrigerator. When I looked at it, it had mold on it. I screwed up my face and was about to throw it away. Grandma stopped me. She told me to just cut out the moldy part. Then, seeing my face was still squinched, she said, "You know, they invented penicillin from mold." Imagination can move from the given reality to a creative possibility.

Think again to the story of Moses's bush-side chat with God. God decreed that he should free the slaves. The God who created us in his own image, as the first book of the Bible says, is the author of liberty, intending for every person to "breathe free."

Professor Walter Bruggemann once observed that the moment of liberation didn't actually begin when Moses told Pharaoh, "Let my people go." And it didn't begin when the plagues eventually forced the Egyptian slave masters to give up. Or when God parted the waters of the Red Sea and set the slaves free. No, the freedom movement began the moment Moses talked to God and began to imagine the *possibility* of a world without slavery.

That's when freedom movements always begin. That's when movements that have in any way helped us humans become more humane begin. Making do reaches fruition when someone dares to imagine another possibility greater than what appears to be the reality.

Jesus said, "Unless you change and become as little children, you will never see the kingdom of heaven." Some years ago I attended a lecture by the late Urban "Terry" Holmes, who was then dean and professor of theology at the School of Theology at the University of the South. His take was that Jesus may well have been referring to a specific characteristic of children—*imagination*. He went on to explain that children have vivid and boundless imaginations. They dwell happily in that space between fantasy and reality. Theirs is often that land of the fairy tale, the cartoon. They fantasize, they imagine, they dream. I think Dr. Holmes was right. To behold the reign of God, that perfect realization of God's peace, God's shalom, God's salaam—the dream of God—we must become as little children. We must imagine and, as you'll see in the next chapter, dream.

The movie *The Hurricane* tells the true story of Rubin "the Hurricane" Carter, one of the great boxers of the last century. More than that, it tells the story of two people whose relationship creates a new world of possibilities that set them both free. Carter was in prison for life for a murder he never committed. Lesra Martin was a Brooklyn teenager who didn't learn to read until he was sixteen years old. The first book he read was Carter's *The Sixteenth Round*, which Carter had written in jail. He writes a letter to Carter and gets a response. After that, he goes to visit him in prison.

In the movie, Carter tells Martin, "We must transcend the places that hold us." Carter transcended his literal prison with his imagination: By writing his book, he freed his mind and spirit. "Every time I sat down to write, I could rise above the walls of this prison," he says. "I could look out over the walls all across the state of New Jersey, and I could see Nelson Mandela in his cell writing his book. I could see Huey. I could see Dostoyevsky. I could see Victor Hugo, Emile Zola."

At the point Lesra visits him, Carter had been in prison for twenty years. All the celebrities who had taken up his cause had given up. But Lesra brings Carter hope—and real possibilities. He convinces a new team of lawyers to involve themselves in Carter's case. It takes five years of hope and hard work, but they win Carter his freedom.

Through writing, Carter transcended, rose above—ascended, as the Bible says—his circumstances, first in spirit and eventually in reality. He imagined, then won his actual freedom. That's key. Because as I've said, making do is not about escaping reality or finding a little wiggle room in the bonds that hold you. It's about rising higher than those bonds so that you have the vantage and strength to break them forever.

The real genius of Grandma, and those of her generation, was that they looked at a problem and found or created a possibility. They took "danger waters," as the slaves used to say, and made them baptismal waters of new life and new possibility.

Ingredient Three: God

For my grandmother and those of her world and generation, God was a given. Not taken for granted, but given. I remember picking her up one day in my adulthood, at which point she was probably in her eighties. She and her friend had to cross a busy street and step up a steep curb in order to get to my car. When they made it, they turned and grabbed each other's arm, saying, "Our God is a good God!" I chuckled and remembered my father teasing Grandma, saying, "You folk talk about the Lord so much you would think he lived next door." God was right there, front and center, all the time. An old hymn says it this way: "O God unseen yet ever near, thy presence may we feel." Or as the Gospel hymn says, "Yes, God is real!"

There's a powerful moment in Lorraine Hansberry's

A Raisin in the Sun. After suffering many hardships and interfamily conflicts and issues, the daughter, Beneatha, in anger lectures her mother.

"Mama, you don't understand. It's all a matter of ideas, and God is just one idea I don't accept. It's not important. I am not going out and be immoral or commit crimes because I don't believe in God. I don't even think about it. It's just that I get tired of Him getting credit for all the things the human race achieves through its own stubborn effort. There simply is no blasted God—there is only man and it is he who makes miracles!"

Her mother pauses and looks at her, clearly processing this internally. Then she hauls off and slaps her daughter. "Now, you say after me, 'in my mother's house there is still God,'" she says. God was a given!

When God is factored into the equation of life, the outcome changes. It has to. My mother was a mathematician. So is my sister. She got the math gene. I didn't, but I do remember this much from high school algebra: In any equation, if you alter one of the factors or variables, you alter the outcome of the equation. That principle is true in chemistry and physics as well. Change one variable and you alter the outcome. It's true in cooking, too. Alter one of the ingredients, or the amount of it, and sometimes you've got a new dish.

When God—that loving benevolence behind creation, whose judgment supersedes all else—is factored into the reality of life and living, something changes for the good. It's not wise to try to predict what that will be or how it will look, but something happens. The given reality is altered by another possibility.

That's why prayer matters—not as magic, like rubbing a rabbit's foot. Prayer matters because when God is brought into the equation of life, something changes. Another possibility emerges.

When I was thirteen, I had an experience like that, and it has stayed with me ever since. The occasion was my aunt Callie's funeral down in Birmingham. Callie was my father's aunt, and her death was the same year my mother passed. The funeral was at the Sixteenth Street Baptist Church, bombed by the KKK just a few years earlier, where she had taught Sunday school.

We drove down in a '67 Chevy Caprice. My father was so proud of that car! It had air-conditioning and an eight-track. We had to listen to Nat King Cole, Frank Sinatra, and Dinah Washington the entire way, which for us kids was torture. We were traveling to a funeral, but everybody was excited because it was our first time down South since segregation's repeal. That meant we could stay at a hotel instead of with family. We took pictures of every corner of that hotel—the sign, the doors, the swimming pool where my sister splashed around. A Black child in a hotel swimming pool was a joyous cause for commemoration.

But transcendence, for me, came at the burial. The

funeral procession pulled up to a small cemetery, in a forgotten place midway between Birmingham and Montgomery. We stepped out of my father's Chevy into that wall of Alabama summer heat, greeted by the shivering buzz of grasshoppers. I wasn't feeling particularly somber or contemplating mortality. I was shaking my head about the fact that my twentysomething cousin was hitting on the funeral director.

Graveside, we were met by an old preacher, a local pastor we'd never met before. He was tall and lanky, like a Black Ichabod Crane, but straight as a rod, like a string was pulling him up toward heaven. He wore a thin black suit with the bright sheen of a thousand ironings. The sun was shining on him, and his suit was shining on us. Around his neck was a giant cross, and in his hands, a giant, soft-covered leather Bible.

When he got to preaching, my ears first heard only noise. Then they adjusted to his dialect, the deepest, most ancient Southern patois I had ever heard. He preached Ezekiel and the Valley of the Dry Bones. I could barely understand individual words, but I was swept up in the rhythm. "Dem dry bones, dem bones, here with the Lord," he said. "Ezekiel hear the word of the Lord. Oh rise up, Ezekiel, rise!" And then he said, "O Callie, Callie hear the word of the Lord. O rise up, Callie, rise."

That voice had a weird power that was not its own. The words seemed conjured up by the spirit of God himself, like the veil between the worlds had slipped. It was primal. You felt it in your bones, that force beyond any one human life or death. We didn't create it, we can't stop it. It's there, and it's the source of love.

I think everybody felt it, because when the preacher said, *"Callie, rise,"* everybody's eyes peered nervously down at the coffin, like we thought it might open and she'd walk out. It was something.

Now, the coffin didn't open up, and Aunt Callie didn't get up, at least not from what we could see. Had she done that, I suspect I would have run from Birmingham back to Buffalo at Olympic speed. But that old preacher did conjure up something. It was an abiding hope, a life-giving conviction that there is a reality that we cannot see.

It was in the booming baritone of his voice, in the rhythm and cadence of his speech, that he somehow was both painting a picture and pointing beyond to that which is greater than us all and all things. He was pointing us in the direction of destiny, to the harbor of the divine. He was pointing us to "Great God Almighty," as the old folk used to say. And in so doing, he was conjuring up, from the old reality of death, a new possibility.

We couldn't see heaven, we couldn't see resurrection, but we could feel its possibility. God had been factored into the equation of our experience and something in reality changed.

That's where and when hope happens—when reality is altered by a new possibility. It's what the Bible calls hoping against hope. And that hope begins the journey of faith, and interestingly enough, all genuine efforts to change for the good. That's what making do can do for you.

WHEN GRANDMA TOLD her stories, there was no undercurrent of anger—at life, at the landowner, or at God. She didn't say "we made do" in a spirit of anger, despair, passive resignation, or naive optimism. She would have been justified if she had, but she didn't. She had her foibles and failings like all of us, but not here. Her life was far more filled with pain and hardship than mine.

And yet, by a spiritual alchemy, I am convinced that she, like many in her generation, discovered the secret of living in spite of hardship, in spite of sickness, in spite of death, in spite of injustice, in spite of oppression, in spite of violence and abuse, and hooded night riders hiding under sheets and burning crosses. She learned the secret that St. Paul, himself writing these words as a prisoner of the Roman Empire, was talking about: "I know what it is to have little, and I know what it is to have plenty. In any and all circumstances I have learned the secret of being well-fed and of going hungry, of having plenty and of being in need. I can do all things through him who strengthens me."[4]

And standing at that kitchen sink, laughing and cooking, Grandma was sharing "the secret" that the Bible was talking about. Could it be that in the bitter bite of greens laced with the sharp tang of vinegar and garlic and neutralized by sugar, in the savory chew of fried chicken stolen from the refrigerator, in the buttery goodness of grits, we find a taste of what the religious traditions often call *ascending*—transcending, rising above and beyond to behold and to experience even a hint of a new possibility?

It's what the old spiritual based on the vision of Jacob in the book of Genesis is about: "We are climbing Jacob's ladder." Making do was how and why they kept climbing. As a mother says to her son in Langston Hughes's poem,

> Don't you fall now—
> For I'se still goin', honey,
> I'se still climbin',
> And life for me ain't been no crystal stair.[5]

My grandma was not unusual. She was a living portrait, a profound and powerful parable for a way of life grounded in the way of love. Thinking back to her cleaning those collard greens, I can see and hear a host of witnesses like her who learned how to love and find life in spite of the titanic power of death, hatred, violence, bigotry, injustice, cruelty, and indifference.

Howard Thurman, the theologian I mentioned earlier, shaped the perspective of Martin Luther King and other Christian civil rights leaders on the intertwining of their faith and their great project. Thurman wrote about his grandmother, a former slave. She remembered two church services for the slaves every Sunday. The first was organized by the master. The authorized preacher would lead worship and give sermons that boiled down to instruction on how God would want you to be a better slave. But after the formal service, slaves would "steal away to Jesus," as part of what the sociologist E. Franklin Frazier called "the invisible institution." There the slave preacher would preach another sermon, one that always ended with these words: "You are not slaves, you are the children of God." No matter what the world and life itself may say or how it may make you feel, you are God's children.

There, the old preacher, like a creative artist, ripped from the givens of reality a new possibility. You are not slaves, you are the children of God. That's making do. And that holds the making of a new and different world for us all.

CHAPTER 4

What Desmond Tutu and Dolly Parton Have in Common

Question: Can love really change the world?

> *Since my early childhood, I've felt like my dreams were the*
> *foundation of my drive to accomplish all the things I love. It*
> *was a dream that made me feel dressed up when I just had*
> *old hand-me-down, ragged clothes . . . Dreams took me*
> *from a shack at the foothills of the Great Smoky*
> *Mountains to Nashville and then to Hollywood.*
> —DOLLY PARTON, *DREAM MORE*

SINCE I WAS a little boy, I have been haunted by the language of *the dream*. I can remember my grandma telling me the stories she had heard about Jubilee Day, when the slaves were freed. "They said it was like a dream," my grandmother said. It was a moment when the impossible became possible. The divine promise made flesh. Free at last!

And yet dreaming, like love, is language that people easily dismiss. Dreams are fanciful, ethereal, naive, or even a setup for failure. Or maybe not. "Dreams" were the chosen language of Archbishop Desmond Tutu. Sometime in the mid-1980s, I caravanned to Columbus, Ohio, to hear Tutu speak. At the time, Nelson Mandela was still in prison in South Africa, without any expectation that he would ever be released. Protesters were out in the streets, in marches that often turned violent, even deadly, because of state-sponsored instigators. The funerals of young people who had dared to stand for freedom became great moments of public protest against apartheid's demonic reign of death and terror. Meanwhile U.S. churches, corporations, and nonprofit agencies with corporate investments were bitterly debating whether disinvestment or "constructive engagement" was the best strategy to bring down the Jericho wall of apartheid.

As Tutu spoke that day, South Africa was nearing what Dr. King had called "midnight." Midnight in the social order is the moment in the process of change when the conflict intensifies to the point that it could go either way. Midnight is the darkest hour. No one knew what would happen, but many feared the bloodstained nightmare of a civil war of Black against White.

Midnight is the darkest hour, but it's also the potential break of a brilliant new dawn. It takes a dreamer such as Tutu to see the dawn coming while it is still dark. Most of the archbishop's speech has long since faded from my memory. But his conclusion, words very similar to these, stuck with me: *I believe that one day South Africa will be free. All of her children—Black, Brown, and colored—all of her children will be free. I believe it not because I can see it but because I believe that God has a dream for South Africa. And this is the God who raised Jesus from the dead. I believe that God has a dream for South Africa because nothing can stop God.*

When Archbishop Tutu spoke of God having a dream for South Africa, he was speaking in the same spirit that Martin Luther King Jr. did at the March on Washington in August 1963, when Dr. King told the world of his dream of an America that would rise up and live out its creed, because all humans are created equal.

The language of a dream is the language of hope. It is the language of reality being changed by a new possibility. It is the miracle progeny of "making do." It is Dolly Parton, as a little girl caring for her siblings in desperate poverty, imagining another reality; being quickened to rise to the top and live fully despite what life has thrown at her. And it is Dolly Parton, later in life, dedicating herself to fighting illiteracy and helping children learn to read and love books to help them, too, dream a better life.

Dreaming—impractical, foolish, impossible dreaming—gave us the very real civil rights movement. Dreaming gave us a South Africa freed from apartheid. Dreaming, as I see it, has saved me and many others from turning to despair and destruction in the darkest days, when evil seems to be winning. Dreams are love's visions—the boundless faith that the world can be remade to look more like what God hoped for his creation.

Time and time again in history, the positive, miraculous—even crazy—energy of dreamers has saved us. In insane times, it's sanity that kills us—the sanity of complicity with the present nightmare. The only people who have ever changed the world or anything for the good have been those who have dared to dream of an alternative reality, another possibility than the one that confronts us day by day.

A Dream Deferred

The year 1968 felt like midnight in America. The war in Vietnam was raging, with horrific casualties among the people of Vietnam, Laos, and Cambodia, and among young American men and women who fought there. Others came home wounded, physically and emotionally. On April 4, 1968, Martin Luther King Jr. was gunned down and murdered at the Lorraine Motel in Memphis, Tennessee.

Dr. King was mortal, fallible, and human just like the rest of us, sinner and saint rolled into one. And yet he embodied what Maya Angelou called "the hopes and the dreams of the slave," and the hope of a nation struggling and yet yearning to live its highest and noblest ideals of freedom, equality, and dignity for all. He was the prophet of love. And then he was gone.

Just five years earlier, President Kennedy had been taken. Also as mortal and fallible as any human being, he yet embodied a youthful idealism and the hope of a nation struggling and yearning to live its highest and most noble ideals.

Malcolm X, too, was the hope of a nation struggling and yet yearning to live its highest and noblest ideals of freedom, equality, and dignity for all. Toward the end of his life, he experienced a life-changing hajj to Mecca, finding a way to affirm his identity as a Black man and as a brother to all people. And then he was assassinated in 1965. It was as if hope was cursed to die on the altar of reality.

There are so many more I could mention: civil rights activists Medgar Evers, James Chaney, Andrew Goodman, Michael Schwerner, Viola Liuzzo, Jonathan Daniels; all taken.

The words of Langston Hughes's 1951 poem "Harlem" seem eerily prescient: "What happens to a dream deferred? . . . Maybe it just sags / like a heavy load. / *Or does it explode?*"[1] When the great dreamer of a new America was killed, the dream seemed deferred. And America exploded. Her cities burned with anger and hope dashed on the altar of reality.

When King was murdered, the despair, hopelessness, and anger moved some folk to destruction. They said, *to hell with love. You see what it gets you?* There were riots in dozens of American cities. Destruction is negative movement. It is the perversion of the dream. In the dark of midnight, many lost sight of love's vision.

A friend of mine in the clergy, now deceased, was serving in the National Guard in 1968. He was called up to quell the riot in Washington, D.C. He often spoke of the inner turmoil he carried, that particularly painful experience of what W.E.B. Du Bois described as the "double-consciousness" of being a Black person in America. My friend loved his country and yet he felt that very country had betrayed him. He was frustrated and angry. If an apostle of love is killed by such hate, why not "burn, baby, burn," as H. Rap Brown once said? But my friend did his duty and tried as best he could to de-escalate the violence.

Still, many others did not. The trauma of King's assassination was devastating. There was a moment after Jesus was killed when some of his followers did not know that he had been raised from the dead. And two of them gave voice to that feeling of hopelessness when they said of Jesus, "We had hoped that he was the one to redeem Israel." Dashed hope is the experience of a nightmare in daylight.

And that's where faith matters. It is there and then that one makes a decision. An old song says it this way: "Over my head, I hear music in the air. There must be a God somewhere." Somehow, love will prevail.

The late Harlem congressman Adam Clayton Powell, in one of the darkest and most painful periods of his life, preached a sermon at Harlem's Abyssinian Baptist Church with the famous line "Keep the faith, baby." Faith is trusting God, or just holding on to God, when your heart is breaking, when it's hard to see, when you don't understand, and even when you're mad at God. Many of the psalms in the Bible are expressions of people hurt, disappointed, angry at life, and even angry with God. At the same time the expression of that hurt and even anger is an expression of faith. It's OK to be angry with God. The anger tends to shift from hurt to hope, but it takes time.

In psychiatrist Elisabeth Kübler-Ross's famous 1969 book *On Death and Dying*, she shared what she had learned from terminally ill patients grieving the end of life. She described moments of denial and avoidance, along with times of bargaining or negotiating with God. But she also saw that frequently, with the support of family, friends, and very often prayer, her patients' inner struggle shifted to a place of acceptance and peace. In my years as a pastor, walking that journey with so many dear souls, parishioners, and my own family, I've seen what she is talking about. Likewise, when Dr. King was killed, many people went on such a journey of anger, denial, bargaining, and acceptance. And for many, acceptance took the form of a radical trust in God that translated into a deeper commitment to the work for which King gave his life.

They dared to dream that the struggle would continue. They dared to believe that, as Dr. King often said, "The moral arc of the universe is long, but it is bent toward justice . . . [and that] . . . truth crushed to earth will rise again."[2] It was midnight. It was long. Evil was real. Death was real. But love is greater: "Mighty waters cannot quench love; rivers cannot sweep it away."[3] So you keep the faith and you stand up for love, no matter what. That's what theologian Paul Tillich called "the courage to be."

MY FATHER ALWAYS encouraged me to get involved. In 1968, the year after my mother's death, I had been volunteering in the campaign of Bobby Kennedy, who was running for president. I remember even as a younger kid, going door-to-door when Arthur O. Eve ran a successful campaign for the state legislature. In our home, *religion* and *politics* weren't dirty words unfit for polite society, and the fight for racial equality was a priority of both. As a child, I took this for granted, but over time I came to see that my father's approach was unusual. The teachings of Jesus of Nazareth, which is to say the way of love, have few vocal disciples in the public square and in politics. (Many of the people calling themselves Christians who have involved themselves in politics don't contribute in a way that looks or sounds anything like Jesus's teachings.) So licking envelopes and going door-to-door for Kennedy was a natural thing for me to be doing at fifteen. And when he won the primary in California, it seemed as if Dr. King's dream might have a chance. But my father woke me up on June 5 into a waking nightmare. He gently told me that Senator Kennedy had been shot and killed the night before.

When Senator Edward Kennedy quoted his brother during the funeral, the words stuck with me, even to this day: "Some see things as they are and ask why. I dream things that never were and ask, why not." Why not a new and better world? Why not, as the Bible says, "a new heaven and a new earth"? Why not the divine dream instead of a man-made nightmare? Why not a society that looks something like the beloved community? Why not?! To be a person of faith is to be the one who says, *Why not?* It is to refuse to accept and acquiesce to the way things often are. It is to pray and work for the way things could be.

That's the hard way of love. Suddenly being "a dreamer" doesn't sound so easy-breezy! In 1967, my mother had been taken. One year later, Dr. King and Senator Kennedy. It might have been reasonable to conclude that the dream was dead. I knew two heroes were dead. It might have been reasonable to be angry and bitter. But with love all around me, I was able to sit with my grief without lashing out. And over time, grief became love, and I came to believe that those deaths were not the victory of the powers that killed them. Growing up as I did in my father's church, I was tethered to the dream. I can remember in Sunday school coming to understand that part of our job as Christians was to right wrongs, first and foremost the evil of segregation. Black parishes weren't disconnected from the struggle, they *were* the struggle—and baked into the work was our belief that good would ultimately prevail. I spent my formative years watching my father and people in our congregation organize in the community, lead and participate in efforts to help the

community of Buffalo, and the nation called America, reflect King's beloved community. I remember local clergy
gathering in our living room to organize buses to take
people to the March on Washington in 1963. I grew up
believing, as John Kennedy said, "that here on earth, God's
work must truly be our own."

Even as a kid, during those years of turmoil, I experienced progress firsthand. In 1963, I was entering fifth
grade. My daily commute to school was at once uneventful
and historic, because for the first time in my life, I was
crossing Main Street, the imaginary dividing line between
Black and White communities in my area of Buffalo. My
old school, in the predominantly Black Fruit Belt neighborhood, had been closed. Our new school was predominantly White, in a predominantly Italian neighborhood.
The system-wide desegregation of Buffalo schools didn't
come until 1972, when Judge John Curtin forced an end
to two decades of foot-dragging, but my father recog-
nized and celebrated this small local beginning. At Sunday school that summer, he called together all the kids
who would be heading to School 76 (now Herman Badillo
Bilingual Academy). He explained that God did not in-
tend for people to be segregated from one another. Now
it was our turn to do the work. We'd be going to a new
school where we'd be the only Black children, and it was
our job to represent well. We were to behave in class and
be model students.

Of course, not a lot of thought was given by administrators or parents about how to support a newly integrated school. Integration was the goal, but what that meant, we're still working out today. Back then they just threw us kids together. For the most part, students and teachers accepted us happily, but there was trouble on the playground. No one would let the non-White kids play ball, and when they did, we'd get shoved out of the way anytime the action came in our direction. It got to the point that a group of girls and boys who had crossed Main Street—a few Black kids, an Asian kid, a Puerto Rican kid, and even one little White girl—got together and decided we needed to get organized for better treatment at recess. It didn't occur to us to involve a teacher. Instead, some of the boys cornered the kid who was responsible for the worst of the bullying—not to beat him up, but to negotiate. "We want to play football, too" was the main message, but we called for a general amnesty (not that we used that word!). Without any allies in sight, he agreed to get his friends to stop messing with us. It actually worked, and for the rest of the year kids mostly got along.

In 1967 I started high school, at Hutchinson Central Technical High School, a.k.a. Hutch-Tech. It was then an all-boys school, similar to what you might call a magnet school. You had to test in. Just as in middle school, I was one of a few Black students. I can remember our first student assembly, looking out into a sea of boys all dressed in shirts and ties—the uniform of engineers at NASA or General Motors. Our school slogan was a quote from Francis Bacon: "Knowledge is power: Skill, Knowledge, Power!"

On the first day of class, after we sang the national anthem and recited the Pledge of Allegiance, the principal took the stage for his opening address. He spoke of what it meant to be a "Tech man." He probably talked about values, standards, and, of course, rules. But what stands out in my memory happened about midway through his talk. He stopped, almost in mid-sentence, and walked off the stage into the audience of students, into the freshman section. I held my breath as he walked in my direction, but he settled himself beside another student: the only person in the entire school who had long hair. The principal made him stand, then pulled his hair into his hands.

"Gentlemen, do you see this? The Tech man looks like an executive, an engineer, a scholar, not like this. You will not enter the school with this hair tomorrow." This isn't an exact quote, but it's pretty close. He was a good principal, and I don't tell this to put him or anybody down. As Walter Cronkite ended the *Evening News*, "That's the way it was."

And yet, in the midst of the conformity and convention, there were teachers who taught us to think. One of these teachers was a man named C. Reid Saunders, a short White guy from Tennessee who always wore a bow tie. His class must have been some kind of experiment, because the few Black students in my grade were all placed there with me. It was the one classroom we sat in where we weren't in the minority. (Who knows what the administration was up to exactly, because transparency was not yet a public or corporate virtue.)

Mr. Saunders taught us what he used to call "the canon of great literature and thought." The reading list was more diverse than you might expect for the time and place. We read Shelley and Keats alongside Langston Hughes and Zora Neale Hurston. We were required to memorize great speeches and orations from the past. "A gentleman must be well versed in many cultures," Mr. Saunders told us, holding up the Harlem Renaissance figure James Weldon Johnson as a model of the well-educated Renaissance man.

It was here that I first thoughtfully investigated the language of the dream. I learned in depth about the poems I had learned as a kid in Sunday school, which turned out to be the work of the great Langston Hughes. Like Johnson, Hughes was a figure of the Harlem Renaissance, the great flourishing of African American art and culture in 1920s New York. Hughes composed his poetry during the height of Jim Crow segregation in America. In much of his work, the dream is a recurring image, theme, and message—and in fact, it was likely Hughes who gave Martin Luther King the scaffolding for his most famous speech, "I Have a Dream." Hughes's dream imagery delivers the language of ascent despite the force of gravity of the way things are. It is, in short, the unshakable language of faith for those who must run an arduous and difficult race in life; Hughes, like my grandmother, knew how to make do: "Hold fast to dreams / For if dreams die / Life is a broken-winged bird / That cannot fly."[4] Hughes understood that the dream of a new world would not be realized without struggle, opposition, and difficulty. The dreamer must have a tenacity summoned not from his or her surroundings, but from the heightened world of his or her imagination.

It was during these high school years that many of us learned the truth of this and committed ourselves to the struggle for a world where love is the ultimate law. Together with Kevin Patterson and David Edmunds, now lifelong friends, we organized the small group of African American students at Hutch-Tech. We had discovered that Black students were being systematically tracked to apply only to historically Black colleges and universities (HBCUs) or military academies. We felt that Black students ought to have the same opportunities and options as anybody else.

After frustrating conversations with school leadership that led nowhere, we went the route of direct action. We organized a peaceful sit-in, contacted the local media, and caused enough of a public stink that the administration was compelled to take out the garbage. From then forward, all students, regardless of race, were encouraged to explore every option to continue their education after graduation.

Now, the bigger world may not have noticed the change,

but all that reading of Langston Hughes in English class had inspired us to dream up a better school and to make it happen. It was in these same years that, thanks to the efforts of many students, the school administration dedicated an entire day to the observance of the first Earth Day.

DREAMING IS POWERFUL STUFF. I'm not alone in feeling it. In 1991, Verna Dozier, a retired English teacher who became an insightful lay theologian and provocative and powerful teacher of the Bible, published a series of her Bible talks and theological reflections under the title *The Dream of God.* It was Dozier who popularized the phrase and mined its biblical origins. She liked to quote Dean Howard Thurman, whom she first encountered at the Howard University chapel on Sundays, and who summarized God's dream very simply: "A friendly world of friendly folk, Beneath a friendly sky." The idea is that God has something better in store for every one of us, for every society, for the global community, and for the entire human family. It's what God had in mind when he first said, "Let there be . . ." anything. It is Martin Luther King's beloved community, where all humans are loved equally, valued equally, respected equally. When it came to moving the world closer to God's dream, Verna believed that institutional religion was much less important than individuals committed to living out the teachings of Jesus of Nazareth.

Interestingly enough, the language of dreaming in the Bible seems to come most strongly into play when people find themselves at the margins, searching for strength "to strive, to seek, to find, and not to yield," as Alfred Lord Tennyson says in "Ulysses." As with Tutu and South Africa, dream language takes on the highest importance when hope seems against the odds of fate and counter to the cultural current. You can see it in the Hebrew prophets with their dreams and visions, which challenged wrong, injustice, and violence. You can see it in the apocalyptic books of the Bible like Daniel and the book of Revelation. When reality seems beyond the point of hope, some people lift up their eyes beyond reality and gift us the dream, from which sparks of hope fly and ignite in those who hear it.

The biblical dream may find its most poetic voice in the poem of the psalmist, likely composed at the end of the Babylonian exile, when Jews who had lived as virtual slaves in a land not their own suddenly experienced their own Jubilee Day, freed: "When the Lord restored the fortunes of Zion, we were like those who dreamed."

How to Change a Negative to a Positive

In the Bible, as today, the language of the dream becomes most essential at midnight, when things are darkest. Change starts with a positive vision. Dreamers understand that we need to change the world with love, not hate.

In his book *Across This Bridge,* the civil rights leader and congressman John Lewis wrote that the civil rights movement, above all, was a work of love. "Roots of love nurtured by a river of faith are a sure protection against many dangers, even the power of military might," he writes. "And I say this not as an idealist who speaks in poetry and platitudes, but as a realist who has faced an army of weapons drawn against me with love as my only defense."

When I told a journalist from TMZ that I believed love is the only way to change the world for the better, he said, "Young adults haven't been around that long. They haven't seen evidence of the effectiveness of love in re-shaping the broader social landscape. They want to know, can this really work?" The truth is, they are not alone in wondering. *Can* it work? That question is always the question, because in the end, a commitment to live love's way is an act of faith. Can it work?

This was the first time I had gotten the question in a political, not personal, context. Parishioners had often asked me to help them stay grounded in love. But now I was being asked whether love was an effective tool to change this world we're living in today. I paused and thought, wanting to make sure of my viewpoint. After all, living through what I had, I understood where he was coming from. And who today hasn't felt the urge to forego love for anger, or even hate, in this time of great violence and injustice in America and elsewhere in the world?

Could it be that getting angry would be more productive than doubling down on love?

My mind raced through history, the times the world has made a real positive shift. I thought about Gandhi and the dismantling of the caste system in India. I thought about the alliance of the NAACP and parents who, driven by love for their children and all children, put an end to the evil of "separate but equal." It didn't take a single ruling, it took patient decades of pressure—but it happened. I thought about the fall of apartheid, and Mandela and Tutu and the Truth and Reconciliation Commission in South Africa. Finally, I answered. "Not only will it work, it's the only thing that will work."

Later, another journalist echoed the question, asking, "Sounds nice, but isn't a world built on love utopian, maybe a little Pollyannaish?" This time I didn't hesitate. I said, "OK, let me do a Dr. Phil on you. How is the way of the world working for you right now? Who's the Pollyanna here?"

We're living, right now, in a world built on selfishness, indifference, and even hatred, and it doesn't look good. What does it get us? Mass shootings, the murder of innocents. Brutal dictatorships. The suppression of ethnic and religious minorities. The mistreatment of refugees. The rise of racism, anti-Semitism, nationalistic nativism, and xenophobia. Fear begins to rule our lives. People are hurting and hating others because they are different. We have wars and rumors of wars. We have an earth that has been exploited to a crisis point, despite the fact that, to quote a protest sign I saw recently, "mass extinction is bad for profit."

What it all adds up to is just that: mutually assured destruction. Now that's insanity. Suddenly a world built on love starts to look like the sane one.

Love builds, hate destroys. We have to stop the madness, and you don't stop the madness with more madness. Dr. King had a dream and, like Verna Dozier later, he knew that the only way to get there was to live into it—to live a life that looked like the world he wanted to create. Only a life of love could open the gates and point the way to the beloved community.

Love is God's way, the moral way, but it's also the only thing that works. It's the rare moment where idealism actually overlaps with pragmatism. People don't think of Jesus as a strategist, but he was a leader who successfully built what was essentially a radical equal rights movement within a brutal empire. You don't do that without being a master strategist. When he said, "Love those who curse you" in the Sermon on the Mount, his famous call for nonviolence, he wasn't just speaking about what kind of behavior his father preferred. He was offering a how-to guide on changing a negative situation to a positive one.

The sermon was delivered to an oppressed people, sharecroppers seething and sometimes rebelling against the Romans. St. Paul, in Romans 12, interprets the sermon not as a call to give up and give in to injustice, but as

another way around it. Love was a way that could help
and heal, lift up and liberate, defang and disarm an empire without hurting and harming. What we call nonviolent resistance, or turning the other cheek, is in fact the
strategic deployment of love. Paul summed up the logic
of this way with the words "Do not be overcome by evil,
but overcome evil with good." That's what Jesus was
teaching. This is what Gandhi would later call "pricking
the conscience"—disarming your oppressor with behavior so loving that he can't help feeling the wrongness of
his hate and opening his mind to new possibilities. And
in the end, that is the only thing that works.

Are you curious about what Paul said it took to overcome evil with good in everyday living? In Romans 12:9–
21, he gave us his own take on the how-to. It's a challenging
list. Paul says to welcome strangers, even enemies, to your
table. To bless those who curse you. You can't think you're
better than anyone else. You don't seek revenge or fight
evil with evil. And while you're doing all that, you have to
be genuine about it. There's no pretending.

I'm not going to lie—it's a tall order. As with dreaming, love stops sounding soft and easy. People come to me
all the time, asking, "How do I stop myself from reacting
in anger? How do I stay with love?"

That's the million-dollar question: How do we keep
our hearts and our actions loving, and our dreams vivid,
as midnight approaches? We do it the same way our heroes did it. People like Martin Luther King, Desmond

Tutu, and Gandhi seem to be superhuman, born into their greatness. But Martin was mortal, fallible, and sinful, too. Gandhi was mortal, fallible, and sinful. Desmond is mortal, fallible, and sinful. What the word *sin* means is "selfishness." So while we are all capable of love, we are equally capable of sin.

Given that these leaders were as human as the rest of us, maybe they weren't born differently, but *lived* differently. They worked harder, longer, at their commitment to love. Courage, faith, love—these all must be cultivated! For love to survive when dreams are deferred, it must be practiced day in, day out. And in the end, living the way of love requires what King called "cosmic companionship." When it's dark on earth, God is the one who whispers, "Say, let me tell you about this dream . . ."

But we have to learn to listen. Dr. King knew this. He understood the discipline it requires. So he asked those who marched alongside him to sign cards that committed them to the Ten Commandments of Nonviolence.[5] Number 10 was specific to marching, but numbers 1 through 9 were reminders of the spiritual principles that King believed would help people stay grounded in the nonviolent way of love. I'm walking you through them here, not as a history lesson, but as a potential framework for your own daily commitment to love. (In the "Love in Action" appendix of this book, I'll walk you through an exercise to create a framework that is entirely your own.)

1. Meditate daily on the teachings and life of Jesus. There is a reason this comes first. Dr. King realized that to walk the way of love, we need to nurture a relationship with the source of love. You can do this according to your chosen tradition or spiritual beliefs, but this first commitment is about connecting with that higher power. It might take the form of a brief reflective walk in fresh air, evening prayer, or a fifty-minute Bible study, but commit to holding space for it, daily.

2. Remember always that the nonviolent movement seeks justice and reconciliation—not victory. Reconciliation, not revenge, is the goal. Again, you don't rise from the madness by adding more madness. Reconciliation and revenge are big concepts, but the truth is that each day brings opportunities to unite or divide; to provoke anger or model compassion.

3. Walk and talk in the manner of love, for God is love. This is a call to be the change you would like to see. Make the dream real by enacting it. (See number 2, above.)

4. Pray daily to be used by God in order that all men might be free. Prayer means many things to many people, but it can simply be a means to move toward a more intentional way of living. The author Elizabeth Gilbert has written that she starts every day by praying to be relieved from the bondage of self. Then she meditates. Then she dances. Then she writes herself a letter from Love. "This is the most important part of my day, when I connect to

Love herself, and ask her what she would have me know today," Gilbert wrote on Instagram.

5. *Sacrifice personal wishes in order that all men might be free.* Recall that the opposite of love isn't hate; it's selfishness. Striving to look outward at the common good whenever possible is about as countercultural as you can get in this country. But that's what *agape* means. It may seem like a lofty demand, but don't let that get in the way of starting somewhere: Can you take fifteen minutes a day to check in with family or a member of your community to find out how they are and whether you can help? Can you commit weekly or monthly time to a goal that benefits others?

6. *Observe with both friend and foe the ordinary rules of courtesy.* If King were writing today, he might add, "even on social media." Before you type a comment or a tweet, take a deep breath. Ask yourself what emotional need the communication is fulfilling—then find a healthier way to satisfy it. Scream into a paper bag, call a friend, say a prayer, take a walk in the sunshine. There *is* another way.

7. *Seek to perform regular service for others and for the world.* This is working the love muscle, as I wrote about earlier. The key is regularity. You don't get stronger by doing it when you feel like it. Make a formal commitment to an individual or organization, because it will help ensure you follow through over time.

8. Refrain from the violence of fist, tongue, or heart. I suspect fist is easy for most of us, but tongue a bit harder, and heart hardest of all. But recognizing that violent thoughts walk us backward from the dream is a significant step. When you have an angry thought, don't judge it. Simply note it—then let it fade from your consciousness.

9. Strive to be in good spiritual and bodily health. This may be the most important one of all. It's the call to put your own oxygen mask on first. Unselfish living doesn't mean ignoring the self or becoming anybody's doormat. We'll talk more about that in the next chapter.

Imagine, if you will, the impact of each and every person on this planet taking the time to define and then live out loving principles. In fact, imagine 50 percent of everybody doing this, and being successful even half the time. Politics, business and commerce, religious life, and community would be transformed.

CHAPTER 5

Love's Call—and Love's Calling

Question: Won't loving everybody make me a doormat?

Love bade me welcome. Yet my soul drew back.
—GEORGE HERBERT, "LOVE (III)"

AFTER FOUR CHAPTERS about love's selfless, even sacrificial way of life, it wouldn't be out of line to feel a bit anxious, or concerned. If I open the door to love's call, will I end up the doormat? I hear many versions of this question: *If I'm focused on the needs of others, won't I lose myself? Should I keep toxic or abusive people in my life at the expense of my own well-being?*

These are all perfectly legitimate questions. But the answer to all of them is *no*. I've come to see that the call of God, the love that bids us welcome, is always a call to become the true you. Not a doormat. The true you. Not an imitation of someone else. The true you: someone made in the image of God, deserving of and receiving love.

There is a Jewish proverb, "Before every person there marches an angel proclaiming, 'Behold, the image of

God.'" Unselfish, sacrificial living isn't about ignoring or denying or destroying yourself. It's about discovering your true self—the self that looks like God—and living life from that grounding. Many people are familiar with a part of Jesus's summary of the law of Moses: You shall love your neighbor as you love yourself. *Yourself.* Loving the self is a required balance. If we fail in that, we fail our neighbor, too. To love your neighbor is to relate to them as someone made in the image of the God. And it is to relate to *yourself* as someone made in the image of the God. It's God, up, down, and all around, and God is love.

The ability to love yourself is intimately related to your capacity to love others. The challenge is creating a life that allows you to fulfill both needs. I often speak of the loving, liberating, life-giving God. Sharing godly love liberates the true self, so that we can more fully *live* and discover that place where "your deep gladness and the world's great hunger meet," as Frederick Buechner put it in *Wishful Thinking: A Theological ABC.*

I don't know exactly *why* it works that way, other than to channel my grandma: "We've got a good God and a good Gospel." But I've seen it happen enough times to be confident in saying it. Perhaps loving others saves us from the confusion, the frustration, and ultimately the neurosis that comes when we try to center the world around ourselves. Or perhaps it allows us to step outside the self enough to see ourselves with some distance, for a better perspective on what's missing. Or maybe when loving ourselves is hard, practicing loving others strengthens the muscle enough to turn the force inward.

All I know is that I have seen the wonderful personal transformations that happen when people start navigating with God's GPS. I've experienced it myself. It was during my college years that I started to be able to answer the question "What do I truly need to be happy?" Or as old Black preachers used to say, "What are you gonna do with your dash?"—that space between the birth date and end date on your tombstone.

MY FATHER WAS an Episcopal priest and a parish pastor, and his father was a Baptist preacher, but it was not the life he particularly wanted for me. Time and again he told me, "You need work that can support a family, but you do what suits you." As college neared, I was finally old enough to understand what a struggle it must have been for my father to support us while paying years of nursing home bills during my mother's illness, all on the meager salary of the rector of a small, largely working-class parish. During those years he took a second job as a substitute teacher, often filling in at public schools, to make ends meet. By the time we kids were getting ready to leave the house, my father must have been one tired man, not that he ever let us see it.

I spent many hours of my childhood preaching to

stuffed animals lined up in mock pews in our attic. Nevertheless, I went to college thinking I might have law or public administration in my future. I hadn't ruled out ordination, but I was in a neutral space. When I landed at Hobart and William Smith Colleges in the early 1970s, the environment was ripe for self-exploration. The counterculture had arrived at liberal arts campuses nationwide.

By that time, pretty much everyone had long hair. As for me, my afro wasn't towering, but it was respectable at least. If my wife, Sharon, had known me then, she'd have called me Frederick Douglass, the way she does now when she thinks it's past time for a trip to the barber.

Hobart and William Smith had only a small number of Black and Latino students at the time, but you could do substantive work in women's studies or third world studies, which was still rare even at liberal arts colleges. I was naturally drawn to economics and political science classes; neither the classwork nor the neckties at Hutch-Tech had turned me into an engineer. Eventually I found myself most interested in religious studies. I was particularly intrigued by leaders and writers whose spirituality and insight contributed to work that brought positive social change. We learned about underground Christian movements, people like Ernst Bloch, an East German who drew Marxist social theory from the book of Revelation in the Bible and saw early Christianity as a revolutionary freedom movement. We read Emerson, Thoreau, Gandhi, and Dr. King. We studied the Bible and reflections on scripture from people like William Stringfellow, James Cone, and others who understood that faith was about both a personal relationship with God and a social one that could motivate change for the greater good. I started to see that the public, social, and political engagement of my father's church wasn't unique or an aberration, but an attempt to follow in the footsteps of Jesus of Nazareth for real.

Meanwhile my world was opening up in other ways I had never imagined. When I walked my dorm hallway, I would be blasted by the thick odor of marijuana and a cacophonous mix of Earth, Wind & Fire, free-jazz saxophonist Pharoah Sanders, and my personal favorite, Isaac Hayes's theme from *Shaft*: "Who is the man that would risk his neck for his brother, man? Shaft! Can ya dig it?" Hashish and reefer were the campus drugs of choice, and I smoked them along with everyone else. I wasn't particularly drawn to being high, but reefer was ubiquitous, and I didn't fight it. It was the '70s, and I was flowing with the current.

That changed one night when I came home to my dorm and found a friend completely out of it, nodding to the point of seeming semiconscious. We tried getting him to stand up, smacking his face, and barely got a response. We all knew what "high" looked like, and this was something else, maybe the result of hashish that was laced with other, nastier drugs. We took him to the infirmary. He ended up spending the night there.

When I got back to the dorm, I remember lying in bed, my thoughts on a loop of anxiety and remorse. I had no idea how close my friend had come to serious illness or even death. Now, I don't think of myself as a mystical person by nature. Some of us are, but I'm not. But lying there, my grandmother's face came into my mental horizon. I thought about all she had gone through in life and how she kept making do, by keeping God and her faith close, "holding on to God's unchanging hand," as the old folk used to say. Then I got down on my knees and prayed.

By the next morning, my friend was clearly going to be OK, but something had changed for me. A night that began with me dancing on my feet at a party ended with me on my knees talking to God. It wasn't so much that I had ever renounced the faith tradition I knew. We each have different journeys. Renouncing God was never an option for me. God was the ultimate given in the world out of which I came. I just accepted that. That's not everyone's story—it just happens to be mine. But God, Jesus, and the spiritual were not on the display screen of my consciousness. If I felt the presence of God in my life, it was more like a computer program running in the background. It's there, it has an effect, but it doesn't require your immediate attention. That had been my personal relationship with the spiritual in life so far.

That night with my friend in the infirmary, my world was shaken by something I didn't see coming. I was cracked open, if you will. Vulnerable. And the program running in the background popped onto my screen. On my knees, I felt God, who the Bible says is love.

A Love Supreme

John Coltrane was arguably one of the greatest jazz artists and composers in American music history. When NPR broadcast a series called "The NPR 100" on the finest works of American music, his album *A Love Supreme* was among them. The album is so good you can find it in the Smithsonian Institution, as a treasure of American history.

Coltrane was born in Hamlet, North Carolina, and raised in High Point. He was a brilliant musician even in childhood. After playing in a U.S. Navy band, he began to play in various bands with musicians like Jimmy Heath, Dizzy Gillespie, Thelonious Monk, and Miles Davis, to name just a few.

But during this time he became addicted to alcohol and heroin, a lethal combination. He became so unreliable, alternating between near catatonic states and moments of sheer brilliance, that in April 1957 Miles Davis fired him from his band.

Soon thereafter, Coltrane became determined to get clean and sober. Rather than entering a treatment facility where he could be supervised, he went cold turkey. He stopped drinking and shooting up, which can be dangerous without proper supervision and care. Withdrawal was a long, horrible, painful, dangerous journey into night: hallucinations, seizures, and terror; stress on his heart, his blood vessels, his brain. And then in time, after he crossed what the slaves call "the danger waters" into freedom, release, the end of night, he reached the light and survived.

Coltrane later composed a musical piece telling the story of his struggle to overcome addiction. It begins with loud, chaotic, wild sounds from his sax. In the background is a haunting melody straining to be heard—but it is all but drowned out by the chaos of the sax. As the music evolves, the chaos continues to do battle with the melody. Over time, the melody wins out. A voice emerges singing words that at first are faint but eventually clear: "A love supreme, a love supreme, a love supreme."

On the jacket to the album he wrote these words: "In the year of 1957 I experienced, by the grace of God, a spiritual awakening, which was to lead me to a richer, fuller, more productive life." The piece itself was titled "A Love Supreme."

My little collegiate "dark journey of the night" was nothing compared with Coltrane's. But it was for me an experience of that same love, the loving and utter reality of the living God. It was an awakening—and I do believe it has led me to a richer, fuller, more productive life. Opening the door to love's call just does that. You find the true you, the you that brings you closer to love.

So when the joint came my way from then on, I passed. Remember, this was college. In the '70s. I didn't become a total teetotaler, but I switched to beer, figuring that at least I knew what was in it. The much bigger shift in my life came after I visited the college chaplain, Durstan Reginald McDonald, whom everybody called Dusty. Dusty became one of my most important mentors. Aside from being chaplain, he taught philosophy and had a Ph.D. from the University of Pennsylvania. Probably in his late forties at the time, Dusty was a married father with a crew cut—in other words, a grown-up. Contrary to the iconic proclamation of the '60s to "never trust anyone over thirty," Dusty was trusted by every kid on campus, from conscientious objectors to conservative fraternity guys.

Dusty helped me arrive at answers in the way a good chaplain does: He listened, asked questions, and maybe made a few suggestions. He never made a conclusion for you, instead helping light the way as you eked out your own path. We had one particularly influential conversation on an airplane, on our way to a student conference. I was still considering law school but starting to think more and more about ordination. I told Dusty about my father's financial struggles. "I've seen what that's like. I don't need to be rich, but maybe I could go to law school and make some money and do good at the same time," I said.

"It's true, you don't get rich by being ordained," he said. "But you'll never starve, either. Your family will have enough to get by." Thinking about my own family again, I realized that even under extreme circumstances, it was true. In the worst crises, we never starved, or even wanted.

"You have to ask yourself what you want out of life. If it isn't money, then maybe having *enough* is enough." This conversation helped me get much clearer on myself. It wasn't my dream to be rich. I knew I wanted to work for a better world. But should it be through law or public administration, or in the church? I meditated and prayed on that question, and I always felt myself coming back to my grandma.

Still, I didn't know the answer until I was writing my senior thesis on King's commitment to nonviolence, on whether it was a tactic or an abiding way of life. I traveled to Boston University, one of King's alma maters, where I was able to pull his bound dissertation and sit with it there in the reading room. Something about being there, in the library he would have used, holding the very pages that he had handed in to his professors, made me feel more connected than ever. King's driving belief was that Jesus's teachings introduced a way of life that could change the world, and the individual, for the better. Changing laws was important, but the real progress, the real moment of stepping into the dream, comes when you change hearts. There was something in me that said, "That's what faith does. That's the faith business." King got that, and I was starting to as well. And so I went to seminary, not to law school. As far as money went, especially in the earliest years of my vocation, we made do, and that was more than enough.

Lift Every Voice

My father may not have encouraged the collar, but all my life he taught me a higher truth: To be who I am, and proud of who I am. In fifth grade, I found a book in the library called *Up from Slavery* by Booker T. Washington. I don't think I knew who he was, but the title and the illustration of Washington as a boy on its cover got my attention. That was my first year being bused over to School 76. Our teacher had taught us how to make paper-bag book covers for our textbooks, and I decided to make a cover for this book. When Daddy saw me reading it, he wanted to know what it was.

"Son, why'd you put a cover on it?" he asked me gently.

"That's what Ms. Lenny taught us to do," I said.

"But I see you haven't covered the other books you got from the library."

I shrugged. I didn't want to tell him the truth—that I wasn't sure what the other kids, mostly White, would think about it.

"Are you ashamed of who you are?" he asked, his tone absent judgment.

My father, who had the same Socratic gift as Dusty, left me with that question, and my burning ears. Was slavery part of my identity to be ashamed of, or something that I could redeem? This was long before I would read the work of the French Algerian psychologist Frantz Fanon and understand the danger of shame. Fanon studied the effects of colonialism and first described the way oppressed people internalize their oppression. Instead of hating slavery and fighting oppression, they come to hate the slave, the self. I took the book cover off.

Self-hatred is an easy trap to fall into, not only for Black Americans but for anyone society doesn't roll out the red carpet for. Self-hate creates a kind of internal schism where we lose the confidence of our own intuition. It's Du Bois's "double-consciousness" all over again.

Somehow, when we come to love ourselves through God's eyes, and through loving others, we become whole again. "Grant your people grace to love what you command and desire what you promise; that, among the swift and varied changes of the world, our hearts may surely there be fixed where true joys are to be found," the prayer book has us ask of God during Lent. When we are at peace with ourselves, our true voice becomes clear and resonant, among the swift and varied changes of the world. We hear the words of our own needs and desires, and can articulate them confidently to others.

My friend and mentor the late Barbara Harris was the first woman bishop of The Episcopal Church and the worldwide Anglican Communion, and a Black woman at that. Prior to her ordination, she had already had two tandem careers, as a civil rights activist and as a public relations representative. Bishop Harris has a stronger sense of identity than maybe anyone I have ever met. It makes her the world's most unapologetic truth-teller and an incredibly courageous preacher. I don't think it's unrelated that she also has, as she would say, an indomitable faith, and with it the unshakable belief that God has no favorites. When she was elected bishop, she told a reporter, "I certainly don't want to be one of the boys. I want to offer my peculiar gifts as a black woman . . . a sensitivity and an awareness that comes out of more than a passing acquaintance with oppression."[1]

Like Bishop Harris, I was fortunate to attend seminary in an age in which The Episcopal Church encourages clergy to preach with their authentic voice—or to be more accurate, however the spirit moves them. When my father first heard me give a sermon, he said, "You preach just like your granddaddy." My granddaddy was a Baptist, with the style and trappings of a fervent revivalist. When my father went to Episcopal seminary, that emotive style was strongly discouraged, in favor of a format that was more lecture-like. And so the church I grew up in, my father's church, was quiet. His sermons were learned reflections. We said you should love the Lord your God with all your heart, soul, mind, and strength, but the subtle message was that this meant first and foremost with your mind. It's not an exaggeration to say that in Anglican culture at that time, displays of emotion were considered a sign of inferior intelligence. My father said that they were actually told that in seminary.

When I entered seminary, the American Episcopal community was awakening to the idea that your real offering as a preacher was the sharing of your genuine self. That self no longer had to imitate an old-fashioned Anglican idea of what a preacher should be. And so I developed my own style over the years, with the help of my parishioners. At my church in Lincoln Heights, which was my second parish, there was a woman, Ms. Saunders, who came without fail to the early service. Like most of the congregation, she was quiet during the service; you might get an "amen" every once in a while. But I always found out afterward if she liked the sermon. She'd effuse, "Oh, you preached this morning, Reverend Curry. You were *preachin'*." If she didn't like it, she'd very pointedly find something else to comment on: "Do you have a new robe on today? How nice." And you really knew you lost her when she said only, "I hope you have a good day, Reverend."

Those days when she said, *"You were preachin',"* I thought a lot about what she meant. She wasn't telling me that she was impressed with the information I had assembled or that I had entertained her. What she meant was that something in that sermon had touched something at her core. That's what truly authentic preaching can do: make the word become flesh and dwell in somebody's life. I try to cut through the rationale to someone's heart, so that you can then walk into the intellectual part of the argument with an open mind. It's not so much about emoting what Michael feels as it is about connecting my energy, and the room's energy, to love's source.

What I've learned is that you can't open someone else's heart without being true to your own. If I hadn't learned this, you probably wouldn't be reading this book, because no one would have asked me to write it. Part of the reason why my appearance at the royal wedding stopped folks in their tracks was that people couldn't believe they were seeing a Black American preacher just being himself in front of an audience of the royal family and the British aristocracy.

When you commit to being yourself in any environment, even your presence can be a powerful corrective. Barbara Harris said it so well: "One way to help combat [systemic racism] is to stand firm and be who you are and to force people, therefore, to deal with you as you really are, and not try to become acceptable to people by being something or someone you are not, in the hope of changing their perception about you. I think you stand up to systemic racism by being true to who you are and what you believe, and what you stand for."[2] Anyone who commits to being a living witness to the way of love—White, Black, or Brown—will have a moment when these words will apply.

My own version of her advice is shorter: *Don't try to be what you ain't.* But that doesn't mean you don't grow and change with life's experiences. When I was ordained in the mid-1970s, I assumed that I would serve exclusively in Black congregations. That's what was done at the time, but it also felt true to my mission: continuing the work of my father, serving the community as a parish priest in neighborhoods and among people who most needed love.

During seminary, I was assigned to St. Luke's, a predominantly Black and West Indian church in New Haven, Connecticut, as an intern, and I was happy there for two years. It was very much like the church I'd grown up in, and I felt at home. I learned much from the rector, Rev. Michael Marrett, about leadership, spirituality, and the ways of prayer, which still support me today.

One of the few Black bishops in The Episcopal Church at that time, Bishop Burgess, was bishop in residence at the seminary and my adviser. He pushed me to try a different path. "You grew up in a church just like St. Luke's. You know that world," he told me. "You need to experience the breadth and depth of the church."

My initial reaction was, honestly, "Uh, why?" Nevertheless I took the opportunity he secured for me at St. Paul's, a much larger church in a fairly well-to-do neighborhood of New Haven. Arthur Walmsley, the rector there, later became bishop of Connecticut. In my own church growing up, we had the bishop's Black chauffeur in the congregation, but it never occurred to me, or anyone else as far as I knew, that there was a future bishop in the congregation!

St. Paul's was a different kind of place, or so it seemed then. It stretched my understanding of what serving The

Episcopal Church might look like. The congregation at St. Paul's was probably three-quarters White and one-quarter Black and Latino. Rev. Arthur Walmsley was White, and the assistant rector was a young Black priest, Rev. Isaac Miller. The diversity of the congregation mirrored a fairly recent shift in the neighborhood, and Arthur, as he was known to most people, was very conscientious of the need for an inclusive ministry that would bring the community together.

How to support a diverse community was a frequent topic of staff meetings, where he genuinely invited us all to offer ideas and insight. Such concerns were fairly new to me, having grown up in the context of the historic Black church. I learned that I could speak my authentic truth while considering carefully the language and delivery that would help land it with whoever was listening.

I noticed another difference at St. Paul's, in how leadership was exercised. Pastors in the churches of my upbringing had nearly unilateral authority. You might call them benevolent dictatorships. Arthur's church was far more democratic, with the lay leadership participating in most of the decision making. I began to see how empowering the congregation in this way built a stronger community. In watching Arthur operate, I saw for the first time that negotiations among various interests didn't have to be about finding compromise—"I'll give you this and take away that"—but about developing a solution that was actually better for everybody.

Still, when I graduated seminary and sought employment, the reality of the time was that churches like St. Paul's were few and far between. I would be rooted back into the Black church world. When my bishop in Buffalo said, "We love you but just don't have anything for you," he was referring to the extremely limited placements beyond Black parishes. And so, my first placement was in a little Black church in Winston-Salem, North Carolina—which turned out to be providential. First, I met my wife, Sharon, while hanging out at the neighborhood funeral home, of all places. And second, it was my congregation there who would bring me back to North Carolina years later, this time as one of its bishops, and then nominate me for presiding bishop and primate, the highest leadership position in the American Episcopal Church—a seat that had never been filled by a Black person. In the span of years between my first parish in 1978 and when I was elected presiding bishop of The Episcopal Church, in 2015, I went through many changes. Of course I did. But I think the world around me changed even more.

In 2016, one year after my election as presiding bishop, the Union of Black Episcopalians (UBE) held a gathering in Christ Church Cathedral in New Orleans. The bishop of Louisiana, Rt. Rev. Morris K. Thompson, had been leading the diocese in deep work around racial justice and reconciliation. Katrina had washed away the surface in New Orleans, revealing a multitude of sins and horrors of the past that were still kicking in the present.

To change the future, you first have to reckon with the past. In the cathedral in New Orleans, as in all Episcopal cathedrals, there's a chair called the bishop's cathedra, which is where only the bishop sits. But the one in New Orleans had troubled origins. It was originally the chair of Bishop Leonidas Polk, a secessionist who, as an ordained clergyman, joined the Confederate Army, becoming General Polk, the "fightin' bishop." The chair was carved and assembled by slaves, and now was a physical artifact of the church's racist past. But rather than throw it out, Bishop Thompson saw an opportunity to reclaim it, to redeem the past and point toward a reconciling future. He invited me to participate in the liturgical tradition of the seating of the bishop. To seat me, the descendant of slaves, in that chair seemed to him to say something that words alone never could.

When the UBE and local congregation gathered there that hot day in July, Thompson opened the service by saying, "Today we gather with the heirs of the African Diaspora, in the Union of Black Episcopalians, to celebrate, to grieve, to confess, and to move a step closer toward God's vision of reconciliation and wholeness."

More than six hundred people of all races filled the cathedral that day. After the procession in, the bishop turned to me and said, "My brother, on behalf of the clergy and people of this diocese, please be seated, that today we may continue the work of reconciliation, that this symbol of authority may be redeemed as a true symbol of unity in this house of worship." And then I sat, in the beautiful wooden chair. I gave the Eucharistic prayer, asking that God unite the whole human people in the bonds of love.

It was a moment of heightened awareness for everybody—awareness of the horror of our history and of the hope that we don't have to be what we were. Me sitting in that chair was welcomed. It was meaningful. Still, it wasn't a moment of giddy happiness. It was a moment of recommitment to the hard work of redemption and reconciliation, which starts with honesty about ourselves and our complicity with the past.

The wise words of the late Maya Angelou in her poem "On the Pulse of the Morning" come to mind:

> So say the Asian, the Hispanic, the Jew,
> The African, the Native American, the Sioux,
> The Catholic, the Muslim, the French, the Greek,
> The Irish, the Rabbi, the Priest, the Sheik,
> The Gay, the Straight, the Preacher,
> The privileged, the homeless, the Teacher . . .
> History, despite its wrenching pain,
> Cannot be unlived, but if faced
> With courage, need not be lived again.[3]

Love's Calling—and Calling

My father once blurted out to me, in a moment of exasperation with a thirteen-year-old, "You know, the Lord didn't put you here just to consume oxygen!" He was right. With every breath, we're inhaling oxygen, and we're exhaling carbon dioxide. You're here to give and to receive, and life is incomplete without doing both. When you know, nurture, and ultimately share your true self, you breathe God's love into every space you inhabit.

What that looks like is different for every person, and it changes over the course of life. But I tell you this, everyone's got a way to give. I will never forget a woman named Ruth Miller. She was the parishioner in my father's church who hemmed and washed the vestments for the acolytes, the kids who assist during services with things like lighting the candles and passing the offering plate. Wanting to be part of my father's services, I became an acolyte when I was five years old. Since they didn't make vestments that small, I spent what felt like a lot of time standing on Ms. Miller's dining room table. She patiently took my measurements and made pleasant conversation. I liked Ms. Miller well enough even at age five, but what really held my fascination was that she had two prosthetic legs, which attached below the knee. She was slow but could get around pretty well.

It wasn't until I got to seminary that she told me her story. In the 1940s, she had lost her legs in a house fire. While she recuperated in the hospital, she fell into a dark depression and was struggling to understand what future she could have without her legs. She didn't know if she'd ever be mobile again. During this time, she was visited by my father's predecessor. "Father Brown," she pleaded, "if only the Lord will heal me, I'll find a way to serve him."

When she got her prosthetic legs, she was delighted just to be able to stand and walk across a room again. Figuring that God had made good on his side of the bargain, she thought seriously about how she would do the same. Ms. Miller made her living as a seamstress, so she volunteered to take charge of the church's vestments, not just for acolytes but for the choir kids, too. Over the years, we all became her children. When I came home from seminary, one Sunday she pulled me close into a hug and shared with me a side of herself I couldn't have understood as a child. "I got prosthetic legs, but you were all my boys. You'll go places I'll never go," she said to me, tearing up with pride. "But your legs are my legs. Wherever you go, I go. God has given me legs I never knew I had." In that moment, I was incredibly moved. Now looking back, I can see that living out her promise, sharing her gifts, had healed her in a way she could never have seen all those years before in her hospital bed.

Selflessly pursuing your calling doesn't always lead a person to serve others directly. I've always loved the film *Chariots of Fire*, which tells the story of two real-life runners in the 1924 Olympics. I've talked to so many people who came to this movie the same way I did: "My father made me watch it." One of the runners depicted, Eric Liddell, is a Scottish Christian who comes from a family who went to China as missionaries. In the movie, his sister tries to convince him that his running is a distraction from serving the Lord. He tells her, "I believe God made me for a purpose, but he also made me fast! And when I run I feel his pleasure." He went on to win Olympic gold— and then returned to China, where he lived until his death at age forty-three.

When you discover your nature and live into it, self-love radiates. Others feel it and benefit from it. Your joy gives you an energy that helps you to love others as yourself. When I was the bishop of North Carolina, I had the pleasure of visiting Botswana in southern Africa to kick off a companion relationship with the Anglican Diocese there. We visited many of the daycare centers for young children operated by the diocese and other churches. This is an area that has been ravaged by AIDS, and many of the children are orphans being raised by extended family members. Many of the children are living with HIV themselves.

The last daycare center on our itinerary was at St. Peter's Church, in an impoverished section of Gaborone, the capital city. We pulled into the courtyard in a van and were greeted by the priest, Father Andrew. I've gotten to know him and his wife in the years since. These two remarkably humble people have dedicated their lives to children in need.

Father Andrew greeted us and took us to the far side of the courtyard where the children were sitting on the grass in the shade. They jumped up to greet us with a song. "Good morning to you, good morning to you," they sang. Father Andrew introduced us. We shared in story time and singing: "If You're Happy and You Know It, Clap Your Hands," "Praise Ye the Lord, Hallelujah." And then we all sang this song together:

> *Jesus loves me, this I know,*
> *for the Bible tells me so.*
> *Little ones to him belong,*
> *they are weak but he is strong.*
> *Yes, Jesus loves me.*
> *Yes, Jesus loves me.*
> *Yes, Jesus loves me.*
> *The Bible tells me so.*

And with that, Father dismissed the children for playtime. Off they went, racing one another to the playground. That is, all except one little girl who was maybe four or five. I had seen that she was sitting in a chair, not on the grass like the others. But what I hadn't noticed was her crutch. Now she very deliberately took it in her hands, staked it in the ground, and pulled herself up out of the seat. Every step looked painful as she slowly made her way across the courtyard to join the other kids.

Father Andrew explained that the daycare director heard about this little girl during one of her regular circuits around the neighborhood. She visited her home, where she was being cared for by her grandparents. Her parents had died from complications of HIV/AIDS. She was bedridden, suffering from undiagnosed polio. The grandparents allowed St. Peter's and the public health service to work with her. Medical treatment, physical therapy, prayer, and love went to work. She went from bed to a wheelchair, which made it possible for her to come to the daycare and be with other children. Now she was out of the wheelchair and walking with the crutch.

We watched her making those slow steps across the courtyard, now understanding that each one was another victory. And then our breath stopped as she fell. But she didn't stay down. With amazing grace and sheer determination, she took that crutch, staked it in the ground, pulled herself up, and kept walking. She fell a second time before she reached the other children. Father Andrew said, "We believe that God has something better in store for every child. And it's our job to help each child find out what that is, and then live."

If that little girl can do it, we can all do it. We all have that duty to ourselves. We all have parts of us that are weak or broken, and parts that are strong. No one is coming to the game in perfect form, and few of us come out of the gate knowing what the goal is. The more we listen to love— let it guide us through life—the faster we find that sweet spot, that intersection where our deep gladness and the world's hunger meet and walk the path of love together.

CHAPTER 6

It's Not Easy

*Question: I'm just a regular person—can
my love have an impact?*

*We cannot do everything, and there is a sense of
liberation in realizing this.
This enables us to do something, and to do it very well.*
—BISHOP KEN UNTENER

IN RICHARD POWERS's Pulitzer Prize–winning novel
The Overstory, one of the characters tells a joke that
goes something like this:

What's the best time to plant a tree? Twenty years ago.

What's the second-best time? Right now.

The best time to plant a seed is now. Change is a long,
slow march heavenward, with as many twists and turns
as there are branches in a growing tree. Accepting that
change doesn't necessarily conform to any human time-
line or plan is the first step. The second step is to stop
worrying about it and get moving.

I have a nine-year term as the presiding bishop of The
Episcopal Church. If you had asked me when I was twenty-

five what I expected I could get done in that time, the answer would have been very different from what I would tell you today. Back then, I would have expected to see some tangible fruit. What I've learned in the intervening years is that my job is only to sow the seeds. That's everyone's job. The error of youth is thinking that you've succeeded—or it's worth contributing—only when you can see, touch, or taste the fruit.

Human progress and change for the good is never linear. "Battles are lost with the same spirit in which they are won," as Walt Whitman wrote. No cross, no crown, as the old saying goes. And so, whatever our effort, whatever we may wish, we might go one step forward, two steps back, two steps forward, then one step back, a detour here, a circling back there, and on and on. The journey is always a struggle. But the movement is always forward, no matter the obstacles.

Now if you ask me why this is the case, I'll answer honestly: I don't know. All I know is that it is. As Frederick Douglass, himself a former slave who won his emancipation and then committed his life to freeing others, put it, "If there is no struggle there is no progress. Those who profess to favor freedom and yet depreciate agitation, are men who want crops without plowing up the ground, they want rain without thunder and lightning. They want the ocean without the awful roar of its many waters."[1]

All human progress and change for the good, whether

individual or social, is the result of struggle, often long and laborious. Our task is to do our task, not to do every task needed for progress to happen. When we accept that, we free ourselves to do what we can, with the time and resources we have. We "keep a-inchin' along, like the po' inchworm," as the spiritual goes. In 2015, in his Christmas homily, Pope Francis sought to express this truth by quoting the words often attributed to the late Óscar Romero, the archbishop of El Salvador, who was killed for his commitment to bettering the lives of the poor in his country. Though Romero didn't write them, they reflect who this great soul was and what he stood for: "We may never see the end results, but that is the difference between the master builder and the worker. We are workers, not master builders, ministers not messiahs. We are prophets of a future not our own."[2]

The distance between you and a historic changemaker such as Mother Teresa, the Dalai Lama, Madame Curie, or Abe Lincoln is not so great as you think. Your job is to do your job, as theirs was to do theirs. God is God. We are human. The God who the Bible says is love knows all and sees all. Meanwhile, we're only human, and as St. Paul says, "We see through a glass, darkly." By the way, when Paul said that, it was in that same great poem to love we talked about earlier.

None of us can know where our witness to love might lead—what light we might bring to the world. Our job is to do our job, and to let God do God's job. Former Morehouse men who were students of the late Benjamin Elijah Mays have told me that he often said in chapel services, "Faith is taking your best step and leaving the rest to God." The only thing we need to know is this: The nature of progress is struggle, and if we give up because victory seems so far away or outside our individual grasp that we can't see it, then we've lost already. Our job is to do our job, and to let God do God's job.

A Step Forward and a Step Back

Accepting our place in the struggle is not an easy lesson to learn. It hasn't been for me. But I suspect it is a necessary life lesson. That may be why the Ten Commandments begin with the words "I am the Lord your God, who brought you out of the land of Egypt, out of the house of slavery; you shall have no other gods before me."[3] I'm thankful for that reminder, right there up front, because the frustration happens when I try to do more than my job and try to be God.

I keep having to learn that lesson anew, so I suspect the schooling will go on for the rest of my life. But my first conscious education in "doing my job, only my job," probably began in the tiny township of Lincoln Heights, Ohio. It was my second assignment as a parish priest, after four years in Winston-Salem. It was 1982. I was approaching thirty years old and married to Sharon. Our little family then was composed of the two of us, our toddler, Rachel, a dog named Bishop, and a cat named Muffin. (Our younger daughter came along later, when we were living in Baltimore.)

My new parish was St. Simon of Cyrene. The name of the parish, a common one for Black churches, turned out to be prophetic. St. Simon was the African in the Bible who picked up the cross and carried it for Jesus. I used to tell the congregation (and myself) all the time, "That's our vocation, to follow him in the struggle for a better world, to pick up the cross when the Lord falls, to follow him in the way of love, even and especially when the way is rough and the going gets tough and the hills are hard to climb," as the song goes. "That's our job now. We are St. Simon of Cyrene."

My godmother, the late Sister Althea Augustine, used to come over to our house on Sunday afternoons to watch NFL or NBA games. One Sunday, after one of those sermons when I reminded everyone that we are St. Simon, she said, "You know, you were baptized in another church called St. Simon the Cyrenian, in Maywood, Illinois."

Good people in Lincoln Heights had been planting seeds of hope long before I ever arrived. The leaders and people of the community had struggled long and hard, often like Sisyphus in the Greek myth, pushing the rock up hill, only to have to do it again and again when it rolled back down. But they also knew, almost intuitively, or as a matter of dogged and determined faith, that the truth of struggle against social, economic, and political forces that seem insurmountable is worth waging because it is for the good. And the good is born of God. And in the end, nothing can stop God. As a friend of mine says, "In the end, love wins!"

Lincoln Heights had come into existence in the 1920s as a Black settlement called Woodlawn Terrace. Folk making their way north had found jobs in nearby factories and stayed. They settled in one place, not because it was the only place, or because they wanted to segregate themselves, but because they were shut out from other places by zoning and redlining. The village where they were able to buy homes had no paved roads, streetlights, fire, police, or public services. So in 1940, residents filed to incorporate, so they could establish their own services and make Lincoln Heights a comfortable community.

Some of their White neighbors weren't happy. They fought the incorporation—but after years of delays and litigation, the residents' struggle paid off. The village won. In 1945, Lincoln Heights became the first all-Black, self-governing township north of the Mason-Dixon Line.

But progress took a step forward and a step back. Because by 1945, two neighboring White communities had been allowed to incorporate in the meantime. They grabbed 90 percent of the land that Lincoln Heights had planned to govern, including the factory parcels. In other words, the tax wealth that could have been Lincoln Heights's was taken. The town saw some good decades during the post–World War II industrial boom but never had a stable tax base. When factories started moving away in the mid-1960s, things fell apart.

Hope comes from surprising places. So here's the twist. Almost since the founding of Lincoln Heights, the kids had the opportunity to attend what I would consider one of the best schools in the country, thanks to two Episcopal nuns named Mother Eva Mary and Sister Beatrice.

Eva Lee Matthews was to the manor born. Her father was a U.S. Supreme Court justice, and she spent her childhood in polite parlors in Cincinnati and Washington, D.C., doing all the things young women did in high society at the time. She hated it. She escaped into a love of literature and eventually found her spiritual calling when her brother became an Episcopal priest. Against her brother's urging, she chose to take her vows, and with her friend Beatrice Henderson, founded a new Episcopal order, the Sisters of the Transfiguration. They started a home for children in need in Cincinnati and eventually moved it to then-rural Glendale, smack next door to Lincoln Heights. When they arrived, they already were providing a home and schooling for sixty-two girls. But they soon got to know their neighbors. And while every other neighbor was fighting Lincoln Heights's efforts at self-improvement tooth and nail, the nuns were looking around, asking themselves, "How can we help? What might this growing community need?"

Being Episcopal nuns, their first answer was a house of

worship. So in 1931, they created the chapel for St. Simon of Cyrene, the town's first parish. From the very beginning the church hosted vocational classes and other community offerings. The second answer was education—the great emancipator and a way for Mother Eva to share the love of literature that meant so much to her. So they started a school, initially modeled on the boarding schools routinely attended in that day by children of wealth.

For decades, that church and school were the primary means of elementary and middle school education for the Lincoln Heights community. It meant that kids had a window into other ways of being than the rough lot their parents had been given. It meant that some kids had hope of one day going to college. It meant that when Gus and Yolande Giovanni moved to Lincoln Heights in 1952, their daughter Nikki was able to receive a quality education, in exactly the kind of environment—loving, curious, spiritual—where a future poet's talent could flourish.

ANYWAY, THAT'S HOW I got to the Heights. That church the sisters founded, St. Simon's, needed a new rector in 1982. It was my mentor Bishop Burgess—the same one who had urged me to intern at predominately White St. Paul's—who now urged me to take this job. He had served there many years before and told me stories about the deep spirituality of the community. He told me that when he was there, plenty of folk couldn't read—although thanks to the nuns, their children could—so even though they'd hold the books, they had all the prayers memorized. "You'll never be more loved as a priest than you are at St. Simon's," he told me.

The Sisters of the Transfiguration were and are a religious community of women who have dedicated their lives to God and following Jesus under vows in community. My godmother, Sister Althea, became a nun in the late 1940s. She had a calling but had a hard time finding a community willing to have a Black Sister. In the Community of the Transfiguration, there was already one; the community had crossed the color line before Jackie Robinson crossed it in baseball. That speaks volumes of who they were and are.

But to give you a picture from the time I served in Lincoln Heights, let me tell you about Sister Mary Luke, one of God's remarkable saints. She was originally from Canada. She was a strong-minded woman passionately committed to the children of Lincoln Heights and their welfare. She cared deeply and didn't suffer fools. She was loved, respected, and even lovingly feared. Word on the street was that under her nun's habit, she was packing. That was more urban legend than literal truth, but she didn't mind that the rumor was out there.

Packing or not, Sister Mary Luke would do absolutely anything to protect the neighborhood's children, and everyone knew it. Hence, I suspect, the legend. One time a dog escaped from a private lot that had become a kind of junkyard. It was just after adult Bible study, at about 8:30 on a Wednesday night, when Mary Luke drove up, slammed on the brakes, and jumped out of her car. "Father, a dog attacked a kid. We're not waiting around for the Lincoln Heights police to do anything. We need to get this dog and clean this up tonight." Then, every bit the robe-clad vigilante, she quoted a psalm: "Let God arise and let his enemy be scattered!"

I jumped in the car—like I had a choice. We spent hours driving around, hunting down that dog. At some point I said, "Sister, what are we going to do if we get it?"

"Don't worry about that," she said, while her head circled around like an owl's. She was going to find that dog, or crash her car doing it.

I thought, Oh man, she's going to shoot that dog! But she didn't, because late that night we gave up. The next day, she got the Humane Society involved, and they captured it. To this day I don't know what we would have done if we had spotted the dog.

Sister Mary Luke was no joke. Some may have been afraid of her, but everybody loved her. And she loved the kids. She has since died, but her memory lives on in the thriving community center she helped build, where children study, play, and are taught how to become young people of faith, dignity, and honor.

Go Far Together

St. Simon's church and school were real points of light
and hope in a community that had struggled through the
1960s, struggled through the '70s, and was still struggling in 1982, when I arrived. With all the factories gone
and no accumulated wealth, it had seen decades of economic decline. The population was around five thousand.
Most residents who could had already moved to places
with more opportunity. But some who could have moved
made decisions to stay and contribute to the community
that had formed them as children.

The church and rectory were in the Upper Heights. It
was down the hill in the Lower Heights where things got
tough. I never felt unsafe, although they warned me that
all my predecessors had been robbed. We never were,
probably thanks to Bishop, our sweet but loud German
shepherd. Our neighbors were good, elderly people, most
old enough to remember better days. Once, there was a
neighborhood alert because an inmate had escaped from
a nearby prison. I looked down the street and saw all
my neighbors, sitting on their porches with their shotguns, waiting. Fortunately for the fugitive, he never came
our way.

Shotguns aside, I felt like I had come home. Like my
childhood neighborhood in Buffalo, this was a historically Black neighborhood centered on a spiritual community. These were folk who believed that witnessing to

Jesus was about living out the teaching and wisdom in their Bibles. These were people who wanted to lift the community up and give Lincoln Heights a future.

We were not a wealthy community or church. We were growing, but finding the money to keep our ministries going was always a struggle. But we labored on. To help out, the Sisters asked me to also serve as chaplain of their girls' boarding school, which was about a mile down the road and is still today an incredible K–8 school, now co-ed. It is genuinely diverse racially, religiously, and socioeconomically. It's a school committed to its Christian tradition for children of all backgrounds. It doesn't just talk the talk of diversity and inclusion. It actually walks the talk of love's way. And children leave educated.

As I got to know the town better, I started thinking about how the church could do more to take all that light and heat beyond the walls of St. Simon's. I figured what we lacked in financial power we might make up in people power. There were two other Episcopal parishes in the area, the Ascension and Holy Trinity Church in Wyoming, and Christ Church in Glendale, both in predominately White communities. Plenty of people in the Heights made their living doing domestic work in Glendale. And then there was the convent, also in Glendale. The priests, Spenser Simrill and Stephen Applegate, and I became friends. We spent time together as clergy, colleagues, and friends. At some point we got into a conversation about the serious needs in the Lincoln Heights community. We realized that none of us could address them on our own, but if we worked together, we might get somewhere.

That kicked off my first real experience of being part of the leadership team seeking to organize a community. As the African saying goes, "Move fast alone, go far together." We did not move fast. Getting the four religious communities and the Lincoln Heights community together was hard work. No one alone had solutions. Everyone had ideas and hopes. But to discover the needs that we together were being called to address took time—to listen, learn, share, and pray. My senior warden, the lay leader of the church, Dr. Willis Holloway, was the mentor who made the whole thing work.

Willis was born and raised in Lincoln Heights, having attended the St. Simon's school. After completing his education elsewhere, he and his wife, Rosie, moved back to Lincoln Heights and raised their family there. He became the principal of the public elementary school, where he had once been a student and then a janitor. Later he had been a catalyzing force in getting the Lincoln Heights schools merged into the neighboring school district, ending the de facto segregation of kids in the Heights.

Willis saved us from stepping on so many land mines. He taught us what I learned later to be basic principles and practices of community organizing. The first step wasn't logistical; it was relational. We spent months getting to know people, meeting key leaders, and mapping out all the people who could contribute to the conversation. Then we brought together people from the Lincoln Heights community, the convent, and the three churches to share stories, identify common concerns, and translate those into agenda items, and eventually strategy and action steps.

Over time we found a focus for our partnership. A bunch of studies backed up what we suspected: that the Heights at that time didn't have any early-childhood education opportunities. The only local daycare option was small, informal in-home places that provided babysitting but not enrichment, which meant that kids started kindergarten already behind their peers in Glendale and Wyoming.

Instead of building a new daycare, we opted to create a network with the existing home daycare providers. Once a provider was vetted and in the network, she received training and a curriculum, along with nutritional guidelines around what to feed the kids. That network bridged a gap, and it existed for years, until more formal daycares came and lessened the need.

Did that daycare network undo the pernicious reality of systemic racism and entrenched poverty? Did Mother Eva and the scores of nuns that came later? No, they didn't. In Lincoln Heights, the struggle continues. Property values have dropped; folks keep leaving for opportunities elsewhere, which maybe says something about progress elsewhere even if it looks bleak back in the Heights. And yet, good people are still there, struggling to make sure every kid has the same opportunities available to kids in places where all the roads are paved and guns don't ring out in the night.

The St. Simon's School closed, but not before it had produced a Nikki Giovanni and a Willis Holloway, to name two. St. Monica's, the community center founded by the sisters, has meanwhile grown and expanded remarkably. In 2019 I paid them a visit and saw hundreds of kids participating in everything from tutoring to mentoring to chess to sports. There are also specific programs to help young boys and girls on their journey to adulthood. The director now is Michael Pearl, who I used to know as Little Mikey when he was a boy participating in our programs at St. Simon's. There are college graduates from Lincoln Heights who got a head start thanks to our day-care network, or who were inspired by something they did at one of our church programs.

In Lincoln Heights, many worked hard to plant seeds. But the truth is, I don't know whether the tree has matured, and maybe it's not my job to know. My job is to plant seeds of love, and to keep on planting, even—or especially—when bad weather comes. It's folly to think I can know the grand plan, how my small action fits into the larger whole. All I can do is check myself, again and again: Do my actions look like love?

If they are truly loving, then they are part of the grand movement of love in the world, which is the movement of God in the world. In the church, I have reminded us that we are part of the movement that Jesus began, the Jesus Movement. And if that is so, we are part of a greater whole. And that means it doesn't all depend on us.

Our Job Is to Do Our Job

On November 9, 2016, the day after the presidential election, I was sitting with a group of younger members of my staff. Some of them were like zombies, not sure whether they could put one foot in front of the other. After a great step forward, many saw this as a devastating step back. I had been as shocked as anyone by the news, but I had been prepared for such a moment by my upbringing. *The struggle continues* were the words a childhood friend of mine always used to sign off letters to me, and those words ran through my head and my heart that morning.

I gathered my staff to try to reset the tone—very gently, because emotions were high, and they were real. "This feels like the end of the world, but it's not," I told them. "It's just the struggle continuing. We didn't see this coming, but it doesn't erase the progress before it. It's just the struggle continuing." Our job is to do our job in God's great movement of love in this world.

And whatever the present loss, that great movement continues. Some years ago now I found myself stranded in an airport during a snowstorm. This was before iPads had arrived to keep me busy, so I purchased a little book to read. It was *Tuesdays with Morrie,* by Mitch Albom, who was then a sports reporter for ESPN and the *Detroit Free Press*. "Morrie" was Morrie Schwartz, one of Mitch's professors from college. After many years apart, they rekindled their friendship. But as it turned out, the professor was diagnosed with amyotrophic lateral sclerosis (ALS), Lou Gehrig's disease. As you probably know, there is no cure for the disease, and it is fatal.

Almost every Tuesday, Mitch would visit Morrie, the student with his professor again. The book is about the wisdom shared and learned from his professor's greatest lecture. Near the end, Morrie told his student one last story.

There was once a wave, "bobbing along in the ocean, having a grand old time." All was well and the wave was enjoying himself. He was just enjoying the wind and the ride, until one day he noticed what was happening to the other waves in front of him. They were crashing against the shore. "My God, this is terrible," the wave said. "Look what's going to happen to me!" Then another wave came along who asked, "Why do you look so sad?" The first wave says, "You don't understand! We're all going to crash! All of us waves are going to be nothing! Isn't it terrible?" The other wave's response: "No, you don't understand. You're not a wave, you're part of the ocean."

The nature of existence is that you get knocked back. You weep, you fuss, you cuss, and you learn from it. Then you get up and go forward again, knowing that you've got the force of the ocean behind you. Progress does happen, but not always when we want it to, or in the way we think it will. But this much I know: If I let God be God, and I do my job in God's economy, that's enough! As St. Paul said, "I planted, Apollos watered, but God gave the growth."[4]

Every once in a while we can see how this works in practice. I saw it a few years ago when I met Hugh Masekela, the South African trumpeter. I was preaching at Howard University's Rankin Chapel, and afterward the dean, Bernard Richardson, approached me. "Hugh Masekela is here and wants to meet you," he said. I was dumbfounded. I had no idea why one of the world's greatest trumpet players would want to meet Michael Curry. My goddaughter Lisa Edmunds had joined me that day, so I signaled to her and we went back together to meet Mr. Masekela.

He was waiting for me back in the vesting area. He threw out his hand, shaking mine vigorously. "Anytime I come across an Anglican bishop, I make sure to meet him," he told me. I was almost a little concerned, since at the time most African Episcopalians were very unhappy with the American church for welcoming gay and lesbian Christians into our church and leadership.

"It was an Anglican archbishop, Trevor Huddleston, who made it possible for me to become who I am today," he told me. Then he launched into a story that knocked me over. It's not often you get to stand next to a legend while he humbly tells you his origin story.

When Hugh was a teenager, he saw an American movie based on a famous jazz trumpeter. When that trumpet came out, he was completely transfixed. The next day, he went to the chaplain of his school, who was Trevor Huddleston, many years before he became a bishop or an archbishop. Huddleston, who at the time was emerging as a major figure in the anti-apartheid movement, had a reputation among the kids: He would do anything he could for you. Hugh said to him, "Father, I want to play the trumpet." Father Huddleston saw the light in his eyes, went to the music store, and got him a trumpet. He realized handing him an instrument wasn't enough, so he then asked the leader of a local brass band to teach him how to play it. Huddleston didn't know what would become of Hugh and his trumpet. All he knew was that he had seen love glimmering and had to do what he could to add heat to its light.

Soon Huddleston had a band of his own, South Africa's first youth orchestra. When Louis Armstrong heard about it, he sent Masekela his own trumpet. Fast-forward a few years and Masekela had written some of South Africa's most beloved protest songs. His music became the heartbeat of the anti-apartheid movement. It was the rhythm that buoyed the marchers down treacherous streets.

Now, when Huddleston handed Hugh that trumpet, he didn't know what would come of it. Huddleston had a lot on his plate. It was around the same time that he and thousands of other volunteers were fighting the bulldozing of Sophiatown, a thriving and diverse area of Johannesburg, and one of the few places where Blacks still owned their own homes and were welcomed members of an up-wardly mobile middle class. The forces of apartheid won that battle. Despite the coordinated and persistent effort of the opposition movement, 110 Black residents of So-phiatown were evicted from their own homes and moved into a cheap government development about ten miles away to preserve the city center for White Afrikaners. Shortly thereafter, Huddleston was recalled to London, probably because word had gotten around that he was a troublemaker.

But we know what happened in South Africa: The struggle continued. Huddleston kept fighting from afar. And eventually it was to the tune of Louis Armstrong's trumpet in Hugh Masekela's hands, backing a choir of marching voices, that Jericho's walls came tumbling down.

It is impossible to know, in the moment, how a small act of goodness will reverberate through time. The notion is empowering and it is frightening—because it means that we're all capable of changing the world, and respon-sible for finding those opportunities to protect, feed, grow, and guide love. We can all plant seeds, though only some of us may be so lucky as to sit in their shade. Since we can't start twenty years ago, the best time to start is today.

CHAPTER 7

Leave No One Behind

*Question: I'm told to love my neighbor,
but who is my neighbor?*

*Love is the responsibility of an I for a
You: in this consists what cannot consist
in any feeling—the equality of all lovers.*
—MARTIN BUBER, *I AND THOU*

ONE OF MY greatest awakenings came on a fairly typical Sunday morning at St. James Episcopal Church in Baltimore, the parish that had called me to be its rector after six joyful years in Lincoln Heights.

At the time, our church was participating in a program sponsored by the Institute for Islamic, Christian, and Jewish Studies to bring together people of all three religions to study the Book of Genesis, a part of the Bible that we all share as Abrahamic faiths. Groups were set up throughout the city bringing people from mosques, synagogues, and churches together to hear and study our shared scriptures as children of the one God. For many, this was our first time in close spiritual dialogue with members of another faith.

The program included speakers from one of the traditions teaching or preaching in one of the other faith communities during worship. And so it was that on this particular Sunday, a woman named Eva was our guest preacher. Warm and soft-spoken, she reminded me of teachers I'd had as a young child, the kind of teacher for whom you always wanted to volunteer to clean the chalkboard erasers. (In my day, that was a fairly involved task that required rounding up all the erasers and taking them to a machine down in the basement that pounded the erasers and put you in the center of a cloud of chalk dust.)

Eva was a prominent member of the Baltimore community who was a survivor of the Holocaust. She came and told her story. To testify. To bear witness.

As she spoke, at first I was hearing her words but not reacting to them. I think I was listening with only my head and not with my heart. Being in charge of the program, I was probably overly focused on making sure everything ran smoothly. I may also have been reacting to what I saw before me: a well-dressed stranger with fine jewelry. She was saying she was a survivor, and yet I could not quite believe this was a woman whom the world had ever mistreated.

And so I was hearing, but perhaps not truly listening, as Eva told her story. It began with a normal, safe, and secure childhood. She practiced her faith and went to school, living as a Jew in Germany in the first half of the twentieth century. Then everything changed. Her world of childhood innocence was shattered by a violent shadow world of bigotry, hatred, racism, and evil. She and her family were forced out of their home.

She then started to tell us about life in the camps, and at one point raised her hand to gesture. And when she raised her hand, her sleeve dropped a bit and I saw it. A number tattooed on her elegant arm.

That's when I finally reacted viscerally. My whole body shuddered, and I was now entirely focused on Eva and her memories. Until then, I had been deceived by my own perception and distracted by things that mattered so much less. And now that I was truly feeling horror, my rational mind kept asking *how*: How could anyone do such evil to anyone else, to any child of God, to any human being, let alone this gentle creature sitting in front of me. *How?*

On one level I knew. I know what Hannah Arendt was talking about when she spoke of "the banality of evil." I had read Reinhold Niebuhr's *Moral Man and Immoral Society* and understood how otherwise good people could be swept up in mob mentality. I knew that my family on my father's side had left Alabama and moved to Ohio to protect their children from the inhumanity of the mob. At that very moment, I was serving in a community in Baltimore that was struggling and suffering because of benign neglect of children and people, as though they didn't matter. Someone once told me that the city had been set up to get people from the suburbs into downtown without ever having to see a ghetto. Subway took you under. Beltway took you around. I-83 took you over. Light rail swiftly moved you by. The system was designed for convenience, but the consequence was division and neglect. Faceless systems and power structures can do horrible things that good and decent people benefit from, often without even knowing. I knew that.

I understood how easy it is for us as individuals to be moral personally, and at the same time be immoral as part of the society, the class, the race, the religion. When the mob does evil, we blame it on the mob, and ignore that we are complicit when we are passive. I knew all of that.

But when Eva raised her hand and that sleeve dropped, exposing that tattoo, I was speechless. I had seen pictures, but this was the first time I had seen the numbers up close, on the frail arm of a hand I had gently shaken. It hit me then as never before: That tattoo was who and what she was to her captors. A number. A thing. An object. An "it." That number rendered her an "it." And when a person, a human child of God, my sister, my brother, my sibling, becomes an *"it"* to society or any of its members, then the unthinkable becomes thinkable and the horrible possible. That's how someone sits by while evil is done.

IN COLLEGE I READ a book called *I and Thou* by the Jewish rabbi and existentialist Martin Buber. The wisdom of the rabbi came home to me in that moment as it never had before. He wrote that there are two possible ways we can relate to the world around us: *I-It* and *I-Thou*. Relate to other people as *Its* and you make yourself the Supreme being—meanwhile, we know that no human is supreme. There's that reverse Copernican revolution all over again. Worse, it makes the *It* your object, a thing instead of a beautiful fellow child of God.

I-Thou is different. *Thou* recognizes the other as an active subject—a human spirit whose truth can be understood only through a relationship. You can't own a *Thou*. You can't stereotype a *Thou*. You can't ignore a *Thou*. You can't throw a *Thou* away. "All real living is meeting," wrote Buber. The loving way to experience others is through a relationship, which requires you to forget what you think you may already know and open yourself to new possibilities.

Stop, look, listen, learn. The key is to pause deliberately, to give yourself time to notice. The Buddhist tradition speaks of the importance of mindfulness. Psalm 46 says it this way: "Be still, and know that I am God." The wisdom of the Sabbath is that it provides the opportunity to stop, pause, and notice the presence of God in the world, God in the other, God in ourselves.

People are not things. No one is an *It*, an object, a thing. In Genesis, the book of the Bible we were studying, God is portrayed as vehemently opposing violence directed at any human being, "for in his own image God made humankind." As Dr. King often said, the human being is of infinite worth and dignity not by vote of parliament or congress, not by edict of prince, potentate, prime minister, or president, but by the divine decree of God.

What has this to do with love? Everything. The Bible says that "God is love." The God who is love created every human child in God's image, of infinite worth and dignity. And it is our love that recognizes and affirms this value of the human person in attitudes and actions that lead to compassionate living.

Love is meant to saturate all levels of human living and existence, because the God who gave us life is love. And as the saying goes, "Everybody is God's somebody."

That means that the answer to the key question of this chapter—who is your neighbor?—is anybody and everybody. As in the tale of the good Samaritan, our neighbor is the person who needs our love. There shall be no *Its*. As the late bishop Edmond Browning, a former presiding bishop of The Episcopal Church, said in 1985, "I want to be very clear: this Church of ours is open to all—there will be no outcasts."

Not leaving anybody behind would turn out to be the defining ethos for my years in Baltimore. William Temple, a former archbishop of Canterbury who argued passionately for the church to prioritize the protection of Jews from the Nazis during the war years, is known for saying that the church is the only society that doesn't exist for the good of its members. I suspect that I was called to serve at St. James because members of the congregation, on some level, knew that to be true and wanted it to be true for them as a church. They wanted to reengage the parish in a loving relationship with God and with the community in Baltimore, a city where many children and people were being ignored and mistreated by the social order. The unremitting suffering of poverty and violence in places like Baltimore is the unthinkable becoming thinkable and possible. The poor in Baltimore were being treated as *Its* instead of as *Thous* by society, and to some degree, by the people of St. James.

When I entered the church on Lafayette Square, I looked out into the pews and saw a sea of Black faces looking back at me. But that's where the superficial similarity to the congregation I had just left behind in Lincoln Heights began and ended. St. James had what you might call a goodly heritage. We all have our challenges in life, but comparatively speaking, all those years the people in Lincoln Heights had lived in the shadow of struggle, St. James had been basking in sunshine. The church had a history of prominent, influential, and prosperous Black parishioners dating back to the early 1820s. I had been told with pride that Thurgood Marshall was baptized at St. James, though we know he was raised in another congregation. The family who founded the *Baltimore Afro-American* newspaper, which was distributed in thirteen cities at its height, went to St. James, along with Pauli Murray, who went on to become the first Black female

Episcopal priest. The church had also benefited from Baltimore's historically solid middle class in decades past. It was a railroad city, so you had Pullman porters, like my grandfather in Yonkers had been. The porters had formed the first Black union in the United States and made decent money. There were also teachers and people with secure government jobs.

When I arrived, the congregation wasn't so different: wonderful people, mostly middle- and upper-middle-class folk—doctors, lawyers, educators. What had changed was Baltimore. Most of the residents with money had left the city and certainly the church's neighborhood, Lafayette Square. This was pretty true of most of the churches in the city. People commuted in from all over the greater Baltimore area, either because they were tied to the church or still had parents nearby. There were some older folk who had never moved, but for the most part, people came from all over.

In West Baltimore, high society had long ago ceded the area to the merely "high." When crack cocaine hit in the 1980s it decimated normal life. In 1988, when I arrived, the place was a war zone. Rival gangs were fighting each other, and they were all fighting the police. It was in 1991 that *Baltimore Sun* reporter David Simon did the reporting that gave birth to the TV show *Homicide*, which was how Baltimore was best known until 2015, when it became known as the place where police beat twenty-five-year-old Freddie Gray to death for carrying a knife.

I was in Baltimore a few years before I found myself in the immediate aftermath of a violent homicide, and saw the dead body hastily covered by police with a sheet. When it happened, I was with a group of Sunday-school kids who were perhaps inwardly afraid but who gawked like it was a live-action movie right in their backyard. During the summers, when we took Sunday-school kids to the park, we sent a maintenance crew out beforehand so they could clean up the needles. Several years later, when the church was struck by lightning and caught fire— more about that soon—media on the scene asked before the flames were even out, "Would St. James leave Baltimore for the suburbs?" I didn't know it at the time, but it was a question that had been on people's minds for a while.

Before I got to St. James, things inside the church walls were about what they always had been. People were faithful in worship and generous toward both the church and the causes they supported with substantial gifts of money and time—for example, taking care of people with HIV and AIDS, who at the time were still ignored and treated as *Its* by so many. But by reputation, the church was defined not by its spiritual life but its thriving social life. There were nine "guilds" that effectively operated as party clubs. Their annual Christmas gatherings were legendary affairs, each guild competing to throw the best bash.

It's all too easy for faith communities to drift slowly toward existing primarily for the good of their members. I've seen that as a parish pastor and as a bishop serving many communities. To the credit of the people at St. James, many were starting to feel a little uncomfortable and spiritually adrift.

A couple of years before I got there, a group of parishioners had decided to reach out to the community. They wanted to throw open the gates and invite in the neighborhood kids, who in their young lives already knew what struggle looked like. Many were growing up with a parent in jail or on the streets, their families trying to get by on food stamps and welfare. These were the kids who, without a lot of obvious alternatives, might in ten years be pallbearers carrying their friends' coffins, to recall the story I told you earlier.

A remarkable woman named Mrs. Bertha Hill had started a breakfast service for kids and brought them to services with her. The group helping her had been growing, but it was still a fairly small effort. There were some who were not pleased. We were mostly an African American congregation, so there was no race issue when it came to inviting the broader community in. Yet even within our community, there were demons dividing us. All human communities have demons, or unhealthy spirits and realities with which they must deal. And ours were distinctions of social and economic class that led to division and distance between the haves and the have-nots.

When I was growing up, the Black middle class and the Black poor all lived in the same neighborhood. As socioeconomic mobility increased, the Black middle class moved into neighborhoods that were still primarily Black, but that left the poor behind. This happened to my family in Buffalo. My early childhood years were in the old-style neighborhood where everybody Black lived together— rich, poor, in between. Then in the mid-'60s, we moved to a nicer neighborhood. Families did that all over the United States. And they did it in Baltimore, which is why hardly any of the parishioners lived in the neighborhood anymore. There were tensions between those who had money and education and those who didn't.

All that said, the people of that church rose up to follow the way of Jesus of Nazareth, whose way is the way of love. One of our most socially prominent women, a retired kindergarten teacher who was married to a physician, began reading to children every day after school. That was the humble beginning of the St. James Academy, which grew to provide academic tutoring and a secure family environment for kids. Every summer, the church operated a camp and Bible school, where we provided free breakfast and lunch. Without that extra coverage, the kids who normally ate free meals at school might have gone hungry during the warmer months.

The Sunday school grew over time to include more than a hundred kids, bringing together children from all backgrounds. Funding all this was not easy. But the guilds stepped up, and soon the annual holiday parties were major fundraisers for all our programs. Friends in other Episcopal churches contributed, too.

The bigger challenge was bringing these kids into the life of the church. It was almost like we were integrating Sunday school. But one relationship at a time, we made it work. Years later, I learned that one of the children who was in that first group of kindergarteners became a master sergeant in the U.S. Army. When he was overseas, serving in Iran and Afghanistan, he would call me to hear a friendly voice. Another one of those children eventually went to college in Raleigh. I'd bump into her in the grocery store there, and get a hug and an update about her life as a nurse. Many of those children, I'm told, still return to St. James every Christmas.

Each step of the way, progress came because one person became committed, and brought along others. And in time, this became part of our life as a church.

Street-Corner Preaching

We also asked ourselves how we could take God's love to the streets. The early 1990s was the peak of the drug wars. Baltimore was the epicenter. There was a homicide every day.

The clergy and churches in our neighborhood had been working together on a variety of efforts to improve the community. There were Macedonia Baptist, Metropolitan United Methodist, St. John's African Methodist Episcopal Church, Star of Bethlehem, and others, all working together. With the help of community organizers, we changed regulations that permitted the presence of a liquor store across the street from William Pinderhughes Elementary School. Kindergarteners didn't need to encounter the kind of behavior that happened outside the store on their way home every day.

Public dealing on street corners was escalating. This was where children were playing and old folks were sitting on their porches. One day, a guy working in the medical examiner's office jokingly said that when he went to a homicide scene, he often sat in his car to start the report. He listened to gospel music on the radio and noticed that every time he rolled his window down, any drug activity that might be going on nearby moved somewhere else.

That led to an idea: What would happen if we started to have street-corner revivals with singing, preaching, and witness?

We loved the idea, but the trouble was that none of us preachers knew how to do it on a street corner. I was Episcopalian, and I knew I didn't. The honest truth was that none of us did. We all preached in pulpits with people in pews. We all had ushers. And unfortunately, churches in our area all had security ministries for Sunday morning, both to watch over people and their parked cars and to protect the offering plate. We were used to preaching in calm, controlled environments where everybody had chosen to come listen. But outside, on street corners where drugs were routinely dealt? That was another story.

The police agreed to come along when we went out.

And fortunately for us, the pastor of the Star of Bethlehem had street-preaching experience. He tutored us in the art of the five-minute sermon, which was a story told in plain language in a voice loud and clear enough to be heard from across the street. We were to leave our typewritten speeches at home—a big step for a lot of us—and speak directly from the heart. And probably the most important thing he told us was this: "Speak out of love, not out of judgment."

As the years went on, we held revivals in the large square that was at the center of the neighborhood. In addition to preaching and singing, we passed out literature for rehab referral and other public health services. And when revival was happening, dealing happened elsewhere.

During the winter holidays, we shifted to Christmas caroling. One night, as we walked the streets near the church with our flashlights, I could sense that enthusiasm was waning. Caroling on the streets isn't like singing in church. In a church, voices bounce off the walls with a resonance that amplifies and improves the sound. A mouse can belt like Patti LaBelle. But on the streets, we got no such lift. Our voices seemed quiet and flat, lost in the air of boarded-up and derelict homes. Still, we stuck with it, determined to share some spirit that night.

We stopped on one block near an alley and began a quiet rendition of "Silent Night," even though we couldn't see a soul. As we neared the finish of the first verse—*"Sleep in heavenly peace"*—we were about to walk on.

And then, from the darkness of the alley, we heard a response. A voice sang out from the darkness finishing the song: "*Sleep in heavenly pea-ace, sle-eep in heavenly peace.*" I experienced surprised elation, but also sadness. Down that alley, someone was listening. And also down that alley, someone was possibly cold, possibly hungry, possibly high. I would never know, because he didn't show his face. And yet, he had responded. Thanks to that unseen neighbor, we understood that even when it didn't seem like it, somebody was listening. That was a beginning, and over the years, a relationship between the community and the churches in the community began to emerge and grow.

I came to see that night as symbolic of the same transition we were going through as an entire congregation—a reawakening toward the community outside our walls, which was leading to a reawakening of the reality of God within and without. It was, I suspect, part of why I was brought to St. James, and it was the hardest work any of us had ever done.

This is hard and necessary work, for all of us. It's easy to contribute money and time to "do good" and help others, whether through compassionate acts of service or by joining the movement for social justice and change. It is far tougher to maintain a humble and dedicated relationship with God and with others, especially others who are not like you. But that kind of relationship—the *I-Thou* relationship—is how we create a new dynamic, where there are no saviors, but only people working together for a better future for the good of all. Without that mutuality, our good acts all too easily replicate and reinforce the status quo. When we draw on the "energies of love," to use Pierre Teilhard de Chardin's phrase, we reconnect with God and others, and in the end, with the whole world.

As that happens, even if episodically, *I-Thou* overcomes *I-It*, and life becomes less about egoistic "me," and more about altruistic "we."

An Unexpected Baptism

If this story has so far felt like Michael Curry arriving in Baltimore to deliver St. James to a higher spiritual plane, get ready for me to step off my pedestal. In the midst of all this work, I was having an *I-Thou* transformation of my own. It took a young man desperate for help to show me I had become like the Pharisee who said to Jesus, "Lord, I thank thee that I am not like other men."

We are all human, and *I-Thou* is not easy. It takes real, disciplined work—and sometimes it takes someone else jolting you back into that way of seeing. It's that voice singing back from the alley that announces, "I'm here! I'm listening!"

I was in my office in the church one day when I answered a knock at the door. It was a young guy, in his early twenties, whose face I didn't recognize. Apparently he had seen our group singing spirituals on the corners.

In fact, he was one of the dealers staring at us from across the street. He asked me if we could sit down and talk. I didn't show it, but I felt myself stiffen with anger. I had spent years now trying to keep kids safe from crossfire, to hold them tight so that the magnet of the streets couldn't pull them away. For all I knew, this guy had killed Dwayne, the young man I buried while his mother wept. He represented everything I was against: selfishness, violence, and exploitation as a way of life.

I took a deep breath and reminded myself what I believed, what I said in so many ways every Sunday. Church was the one place where everyone was welcome. Everyone who walked through the doors was a *Thou*. I invited him to sit, but it was an intellectual decision. My gut was still screaming at me that this guy was no good and undeserving. Even unredeemable. Still another part of me was nervous that we had ticked someone off, and this guy was here to deliver the message.

"I want out." Those were the exact words he used. They tumbled out of him the second he sat down. I said, "Tell me what you mean by *out*." Eddie, we'll call him, wanted out of the drug world and wondered if I could help him. Thinking practically, I asked about social services, places he might go. He shot them all down. None of them would protect him from his gang, he said. He was in too deep. I naively asked if he could enter the Witness Protection Program. He laughed and shook his head, saying, "You've been watching too much television."

That was the truth. I knew plenty firsthand about the casualties left by drug dealers, but I had spent very little time learning about them or their lives, other than the sensationalized, violent images on TV. In all our efforts to impact the drug culture, talking to the dealers had not occurred to us. We were afraid of them.

Eddie told me a little bit about his life that day. When he asked if he could come back, I said yes, without really knowing why. We made an appointment the following week, and he not only showed up for it, but he showed up on time. I thought to myself, this guy is serious. Over several months of covert meetings, he told me more—about growing up with his mother and his grandmother. He never mentioned a father. I shared some of my story, too. The more I came to know his background and to know him, the more I realized that we weren't very different at all, and it became harder and harder to dislike him. Eddie wasn't a drug dealer; he was a person, a child of God, like me. I was now in a relationship with him—and the result was love, whether or not I saw it coming or even wanted it.

One day, he said, "Tell me about Jesus." I'm embarrassed to say that over the course of several meetings, I had never brought up Jesus. That says something about how frozen and conflicted I was, since, having read more than halfway through this book, you might have noticed that Jesus is a strong presence in everything I do. Yet I hadn't offered to pray with this man or for him. I hadn't suggested he read the Bible. When he finally asked to hear about Jesus, I was surprised—despite the fact that he had walked himself into a church week after week to meet with a man wearing a collar. But all I could see at first was a drug dealer, and what's a drug dealer got to do with Jesus?

So we started talking about the Son of God. Initially, I wondered what the point was, given the life he was living. But eventually I understood what he seemed to have known instinctively. His spiritual emancipation might need to come first. It seemed like he was stuck, but here was a point of departure that was in his control. Maybe it could lead to emancipation in other ways.

We began a deep exploration of the Christian faith. We read and studied Scripture together. We walked through parts of the New Testament, reading the key Gospel passages that help reveal a real picture of Jesus. Then we worked through what it meant to follow him. Eddie had never been to Sunday school or church, so he hung on every word. It was all completely new to him—and that made it new for me. To borrow from the progressive theologian Marcus Borg, I met Jesus again for the first time, from a person who was seeking salvation in a very real and immediate way.

One day he said, "OK, what do I have to do to seal the deal?" That led us to talk about baptism. The baptism vows go like this: *Do you renounce Satan and all the forces of wickedness? Do you turn to Jesus Christ and accept him as your Savior? Will you follow him as your Lord?"* He asked to be baptized, understanding that renouncing evil would require significant life changes. Because he didn't want it to be public, we planned a private ceremony. I had done very few adult baptisms, and this one required of the recipient a level of courage that I had never experienced in a church before. Here was someone who was making promises that could put his life in jeopardy. Eddie was very serious about the stakes. "You are sealed by the Holy Spirit in baptism and marked as Christ's own forever," I said to him, speaking the words of the liturgy after anointing his forehead with oil. Never before had I trembled or felt myself tearing up during baptism, but I did that day. Never before had I looked into eyes gazing at me with such intensity.

The New Testament speaks of baptism as the dying of self; an old self dies and a new one rises to life. This was not just a ceremony. Someone was dying and rising that day.

After his baptism, Eddie called me every so often to check in, but I lost track of him when I left Baltimore a few years later. I don't know whether he is dead or alive. I suspect he left Baltimore for another city, but I'll never know. What I do know is that he belongs to Jesus, not to the dealers. Whatever happened, he found his way out. Eddie belongs to Jesus. He belongs to God. And what the world didn't give, the world can't take away. An old hymn says it best: "O love that will not let me go. I rest my weary soul in thee. I give thee back the life I owe. That in thine oceans depth may richer, fuller be."

An Accident of Nature and an Act of God

Five years after I arrived at St. James, a thunderstorm ripped through the city and the church's pentacle was struck by lightning. It was 7:09 in the evening on Father's Day. I remember the time so exactly because the clock on the tower stopped working when the building was struck. The entire roof caught fire. The building was an old stone Gothic structure, but the roof, like the one in Notre Dame, was a wood truss system. It all burned. Everybody stood outside, watching helplessly. People were crying. Another good, lasting part of the neighborhood seemed to be disappearing before our eyes, in what the insurance paperwork would describe as an act of God. To some it felt as if this were the final curse.

The roof was blazing when the fire chief walked up to me. "We've got to make a decision. If you don't create another source of oxygen, the gas inside is going to build up, and it could blow out all the windows, maybe even the entire building." He pointed to the largest and most beautiful of all the windows, a rose stained-glass window that decorated the front of the church. "I need to break that window to let in the air. Do I have your permission?"

I didn't think. I just said, "You got to do what you've

got to do. Just do it. Break it." They did, and it was the beginning of the end of the fire. The roof was gone, but destroying that window saved the building.

In the midst of all the chaos, a reporter came up and asked me about St. James's future. He said, "You're going to get insurance money undoubtedly. Will the church consider leaving the city?" As the reporter talked, I noticed a neighborhood kid named Robbie looking straight at me. He was listening for my answer, his eyes scared and confused.

The reporter's question wasn't crazy. Many other churches and people had left the city and others like it in the United States. "The city" then stood for every intractable problem in America. The city was where crime was skyrocketing. Where drugs were festering. Where schools were struggling. Leave the city and you could leave all those problems behind, for a nice house and some green grass in a good school district. Leave the city and the city became someone else's problem.

But then there was that little boy. If the church left the city, we'd be leaving him behind. Worse, we'd be taking hope with us. Standing there in the light of the fire, I knew that there was no choice. The church is the only society that exists primarily for those who are not its members. We were part of something much greater than ourselves, and we wouldn't and couldn't leave anyone behind. The problems here were our problems, and we would not look away. The slaves sang it this way: "I shall not be moved. Just like a tree, planted by the water, I shall not be moved."

I made a decision in that moment. "St. James is committed to the city. We are not leaving. We will rebuild right here," I said, loud enough so that the reporter wasn't the only one who heard me. I didn't consult with anyone, but I knew the congregation was behind me.

At that point, Robbie tugged at my sleeve. "Father, Father."

"Robbie, the church isn't going anywhere."

"I know. But Father, I left my confirmation essay in the tower balcony. Do I have to redo it before confirmation?"

"Well, that beats the dog ate my homework," I told him, laughing. He was confirmed two weeks later. He eventually went to the Air Force Academy and became a pilot who serves our country to this day.

THE NEXT TWO YEARS, during rebuilding, might have been the best years we had at St. James. We used the parish hall to worship in, which meant that we were stripped down. There were no beautiful stained-glass windows or finely carved wood pews and altar. Gone were all the comforts, and pretense, that dress up the Sunday experience. It was just four walls, the prayer books, and us. Every service, the rows of metal folding chairs were filled to capacity. Eventually I did request one small extra, asking the vestry, "Can we please pad these chairs? I like to keep folks in church a little while, and I would like them to be comfortable."

All our work in the past years had been to strip the church back to its essence, and in some strange way, the fire had finished that work. Maybe it was an act of God. We no longer needed the dramatic lighting. The room was lit up because we were connected to the primal source, to the God the Bible says is love. Everyone could feel it, and everyone was in awe.

The church was just a church. And yet it was more. It was rebuilt by hands that were Protestant, Catholic, Jewish, and Muslim. The entire project was managed by a minority-owned firm where White and Black employees worked together. One of the brothers who rebuilt the baptismal font was from Italy. The owner of the company who laid the new floor and carpets was Armenian. The painters were Russian. Many of the workers who performed skilled and unskilled labor came from the neighborhood.

Here was a church, here was a building. Or here was a monument to what is possible when love is our guide. Here was a recommitment to not leave anyone behind, to an America that equally welcomed all of God's children.

When we finally moved into the rebuilt church, the Gospel reading that week was from Luke. Soon after the resurrection, Jesus tells the disciples, "Stay in the city until you are clothed with power from on high."[1] We were there to stay.

I had read that in Britain, between 1940 and 1942, all the church bells in the country had been silenced so that they could be used as alarms if Germany invaded. After the decisive victory in the Battle of El Alamein in November 1942, the turning point in the war, Churchill called for all the bells in Britain to be rung to celebrate. The war was not over, but a great victory had been won.

"And now, here in Baltimore, the bells of this church are going to ring again. This part of the war is over," I told the people who filled the seats that day. When I arrived in Baltimore, we had been about 250 members strong. Now I looked out at a congregation of more than 400.

St. James had crossed into a new phase of its journey. Just like a tree, planted by the water, it would not be moved. Baltimore's problems were everyone's problems, and we would not turn away.

When, several years later, I learned that I'd be moving into my own next phase, called to become a bishop of North Carolina, I looked out into the pews on my final Sunday at St. James. I saw an entirely different congregation looking back at me. Throughout the church were children from the neighborhood. They were no longer a few handfuls crammed into a few pews near the front. Some were with their own parents, and many others were seated with families to whom they had become close.

They were known and loved. The lightning strike had been an act of nature. The community that was emerging was an act of God, creating in our midst, if just for a while, something resembling the beloved community intended by God for the whole human family and all of creation.

CHAPTER 8

When the Spirit Reworks You

Question: What if love reveals me to be a hypocrite?

THERE WILL BE a time when God's GPS points you in a direction that makes people uncomfortable. It may make *you* uncomfortable. The evolution of long-held beliefs can be a spiritual earthquake; the ground beneath us shaking, the very fault lines of our identity shifting and seeking to resettle. But if we can make it through, we find the reward: not an easy journey but a share of what the Bible calls "peace that passes all understanding," the peace of knowing we are living love's way, without contradiction.

For the first two decades of my calling, God's GPS didn't send me down any seismic paths. You could say I had it easy. There were challenges that come with living and hopefully learning. But from day one, I moved forward with the loving support and encouragement of my family and community. My work as a parish priest continued the values and work of my father and everyone who had ever loved me my entire life. I felt fulfilled, and the people I served were generous with their appreciation. I knew I was blessed. I worked hard, but was more or less walking the path of least resistance.

In 2000, my calling, and with it my life, changed shape. When I got the phone call that I was on the short list of nominees to become a bishop of North Carolina, I didn't take my name out of the hat. I felt ready for a new challenge, although for what, I didn't yet know. But I had a sense that a significant chapter in the work in Baltimore had concluded.

At first, I didn't think that I would be elected. Probably most people didn't. After all, neither North Carolina nor any Southern diocese had ever had a Black diocesan bishop. On top of that, I was (and am) an emotive preacher who couldn't stop talking about Jesus of Nazareth and his way of love, which was not historically "on brand" for perceptions about The Episcopal Church. But somehow, to my genuine surprise, I was elected. Some years later a colleague who was present at the vote said that I was elected by an unlikely alliance of evangelical-leaning people and social justice–leaning people, with both groups left wondering why they were voting for the same person. It took eleven separate votes to get the necessary majority, but they got there.

I think I waited until I knew I had been elected to admit to myself that I really had hoped this new door would open. A month or so before, all the nominees had spent a number of days meeting the people of the diocese in person, traveling to each town and parish to answer questions in town hall meetings and smaller group settings. Toward the end of the tour I said to my wife, "I really enjoyed that." She answered, "I knew you would."

Without my wife, Sharon, in fact, I never would have even applied. A year before, when the letter had first arrived at the church office in Baltimore inviting me to apply, I didn't consider it seriously at all. At best, my candidacy for bishop in one of our Southern dioceses would be a symbolic knocking at the door. And there is a role for that. But in my mind, I simply would never be elected. So I threw the letter out.

My secretary, Lenora Savage, had seen the letter and called Sharon. When I got home, she sat me down and we talked. Sharon wasn't thinking so much about my career but about this being an opportunity for her to go home and be close to family. She is a North Carolina Tar Heel born and bred, and we had always planned to retire there. She had grown up in Winston-Salem, where we met. Her father's family, the Jones clan, was living in the Raleigh-Durham and Chapel Hill areas. This would be a much-desired homecoming.

She then laid it on thick: You don't have anything to lose. You might help to crack open the door for someone else down the road. And besides, who knows. Your grandma is from there. Maybe the ancestors can help, she said with a smile.

I had once expected to spend my life as a parish priest

but had reached a point where moving into a different kind of leadership felt right. Here was a chance to refocus not just a parish but an entire diocese of some fifty thousand baptized folk on taking Jesus's love out of the pews and into their lives, as neighbors and citizens. And to do it in the South just brought me further into the work of reconciliation I had always been doing. My family and I excitedly packed our things for the big move from Baltimore to Raleigh.

I had no idea that, as right as the road was, we were heading into my first major earthquake. But there was my plan, and there was God's plan.

I had barely unpacked the books in my office when a man named Robert Wright came to speak with me. Robert was a prominent Episcopalian in North Carolina who would eventually become a beloved friend and serve as the diocese's treasurer. In truth, the books were probably on the shelves that day, but when it came to stepping into this new leadership role, it was as if everything was still in moving boxes. I was as green as could be.

Robert shared with me that he was a gay man who had been with his partner, Lee Thomas, since 1983. Lee was also an active member in their Episcopal parish, where they had been out as a couple since they'd met. He had come to ask me a very direct question: As North Carolina's new bishop, would I support the blessing of same-sex unions and the ordination of partnered gay and lesbian priests?

To give some context, this was 2000. In 1996, President Clinton had signed the Defense of Marriage Act (DOMA), which defined marriage as between a man and a woman, and allowed states to refuse to recognize same-sex marriages. Vermont was the only state to recognize civil unions, and many states were reactively passing their own versions of DOMA to "protect" the institution of marriage.

As for The Episcopal Church, the language of welcome for homosexual Christians was in place since back in the 1970s, when our General Convention had voted to recognize that "homosexual persons are children of God who have a full and equal claim with all other persons upon the love, acceptance, and pastoral concern and care of the church." That said, same-sex unions were not sanctioned. In 1994, the canons for ordination of priests ruled out discrimination on the basis of sexual orientation. Nevertheless, in most dioceses, gay and lesbian individuals who were openly in a relationship weren't eligible to be ordained.

The policy I had inherited in North Carolina was that if a priest was married, which at that time meant to a person of the opposite sex, they had to practice fidelity. If a priest was single, they had to practice celibacy. Since gays and lesbians were not allowed to marry, that meant they were shut out from ordination unless they were celibate.

My predecessor in office and fellow bishops in the diocese at the time had worked to change this, but to little avail. There was a quiet underground movement among a few clergy to bless same-sex couples privately in their homes, as an act of pastoral and spiritual care. And often there was a kind of "don't ask, don't tell" practical reality in parts of the church.

We humans are walking bundles of contradictions. I know that I am, and experience suggests that I'm not alone in that. The Hebrew prophet Jeremiah grasped this complexity in the human spirit when he wrote that "the heart is devious above all else."[1] As people often describe relationships on Facebook, "It's complicated." It is and we are.

THAT DAY IN MY OFFICE, a good man had come to me, asking for my commitment to right what he saw as a fundamental wrong. If the church believed that all people are created equal in "the image of God," as the Bible says, then how could the current policy stand? I answered him honestly. On the issue of ordination, I was unconflicted. I believed openly gay priests should be welcomed in our church. I say *openly* because we all knew we already had plenty of gay priests in the church, but they were being forced to hide their sexuality. But I also felt I needed to obey the policy and practice of the diocese, which meant that every person seeking ordination had to state their willingness to be faithful if married and chaste if not. I wanted to change the policy, but I wanted The Episcopal Church to change it together, rather than have individual bishops and dioceses moving forward on their own. I didn't yet know how to make it happen, but I was ready to commit to figuring it out.

Meanwhile, I was open with Robert that I had not thought through the public blessings of same-sex unions. "Brother, I'm not there yet," I told him. I asked him to stay with me, give me some time, and keep talking with me. And he did.

The fact was, I had grown up in a church community that did not approve of homosexuality. The way they expressed that was in silence. There was no call against it in the pulpit, but there wasn't anyone telling us "love is love is love," either.

By the time I got to seminary in the mid-'70s, I had classmates who were out, but it still wasn't something people talked much about. I wasn't inclined to be publicly open-minded about it, and I didn't have anybody pushing me on the issue.

By 2000, despite all the polite silence, experience and friendships had long taught me that gays and lesbians were as Christian as anybody else. Still, when it came to the public blessing of unions (marriage wasn't yet on the table), I was stuck in the unspoken disapproval of my upbringing. Homosexuality happened behind closed doors, not at the altar.

And yet, during that same upbringing, as I shared earlier, "love your neighbor" was held up constantly, forcefully, as a core value and commitment. That conviction fueled the civil rights movement that had given me birth. I heard it all the time. But somehow it hadn't occurred to me that that truth must be true for gay and lesbian friends in every respect.

As a bishop, I made a solemn vow to "guard the faith, unity, and discipline of the Church." I had also vowed to "be merciful to all, show compassion to the poor and strangers, and defend those who have no helper." I was beginning to see that obedience to the letter and the spirit of both of those vows was leading me to a real contradiction.

I also knew I was a Black man holding a brand-new public leadership position in a predominately White church, in a Southern state. I love North Carolina, and I'll be buried there one day, but we had history, as they say. The pragmatist and the idealist were in conflict within me.

We all like to think of ourselves as paragons of virtue and intimations of perfection. But none of us are. And I know that I'm not. We're works in progress, hopefully. That means we've got to grow and learn and evolve. We have to be willing to be wrong. Paul gave us some pretty good advice on the subject: "I press toward the mark for the prize of the high calling of God in Christ Jesus. Let us therefore, as many as be perfect, be thus minded: and if in anything ye be otherwise minded, God shall reveal even this unto you."[2]

None of us can be perfect. Accepting that is a great opening to letting God be God in our lives. As that happens, though change still requires grace and sheer grit, hard-won breakthroughs and pushing back, somehow the spirit of God's love breathes through us, constantly making us new.

Robert's visit and our ongoing friendship kicked off a long period of introspection, Bible study, and prayer regarding my beliefs around homosexuality and the church. Meanwhile, there was still a gap between my personal conviction and my public commitment. Robert heightened that tension in a gentle, loving, yet clear way.

In my years as a parish priest, I had ministered to all, and the issue of same-sex marriage or ordination hadn't come up directly. Now that I was an elected leader, with broader participation in the decision making of the entire Episcopal Church, I could no longer pretend that I wasn't part of the problem. Regarding ordination, I was enforcing a policy in North Carolina that I didn't believe in. By not ordaining "out" priests, we were hurting good people in Jesus's name. And yet, as an elected leader, I had a responsibility to respect where the church sat on the issue. I felt stuck.

As always when I'm struggling internally, I felt it in my stomach. I didn't feel good or settled. It was a feeling I don't think I'd had since I dropped to my knees in my college dorm room, to pray for my friend in the college infirmary. Howard Thurman had the insight that the struggle for convergence between head and heart is the struggle for spiritual maturity. I was living that struggle.

When it came to same-sex blessings, I no longer had

the selfish luxury of shrugging away the inconsistency of my position. If I was wrong on the issue, I was actively hurting people. It meant that whatever we might be saying, my church did not look like God, who the Bible says is love.

As I worked through my feelings, I thought back to our organist in Lincoln Heights, a talented musician named Jason. He had grown up in St. Simon's, and his mother was actively involved in our ministry. When he came in to interview for the position, he said, "Father, I need you to know I'm a gay man." I don't know if he sensed some negative reaction on my part, but he rushed to reassure me. "Don't worry, I'm not going to hit on you or on anybody at church."

He went on to tell me that he was involved in advocacy work. "I'd never do anything to embarrass the church, but I need you to know that's part of who I am."

I had decided then that people matter more than any principle. They are the principle. I hadn't yet dug into the theology of it, but I always thought about Jesus's response when he was in trouble for healing people on the Sabbath: "God created the Sabbath for men, not men for the Sabbath." That said, I honestly don't know if I might have reacted differently if his mother hadn't been part of our church.

Jason turned out to be a great organist. He'd come to me, as excited as a child. "Oh, Father, I've got something great for this Sunday! Just you wait!" he'd say.

I stopped thinking about Jason's sexuality. Then he contracted AIDS. There was no hiding this from the congregation, but despite their dim view of homosexuality, it didn't seem to matter. Jason was loved. When he came to church with lesions on his face, they hugged him tighter. He played the organ until he was too sick to do it, and when he died, he was mourned by everyone. In a community where everyone didn't share the same view, we didn't engage in conversations about human sexuality generally or homosexuality particularly. But Jason's public activism for equal rights was not a secret. Everyone knew Jason and everyone cared about Jason. He was part of the community and the community was part of him. Our love for each other moved us to a more profound level of human relationship. The world didn't change, but it was a step, and not an insignificant one.

Years later, when I was in Baltimore, I performed many funerals for young men who had died from AIDS complications. The congregation there was actively helping care for men with AIDS, so that they could be in their homes instead of hospitals. The founding musician in our gospel choir was a gay man who had been shunned by his family. St. James took him in, and when he contracted AIDS, they cared for him until his death.

At the time, I believed our behavior was loving all along. But now? I hadn't thought much about the formal position of the church, or how our silence on these issues had hurt Jason and others. Jason knew we loved him, but he also knew the church didn't condone his sexuality. He knew that if he had a partner, many would be uncomfortable if he brought him to church. If he had asked me to bless a union with the person he loved, I don't know if I would have been able to say yes.

I spent a great deal of time during this period reading the Bible. I noticed that the passages dealing with homosexuality didn't reflect the lives of people like Robert, who had a longstanding relationship with a loving and committed partner. It didn't reflect the lives of gay Christians who had contributed so much to my life and the lives of others. The theologian Karl Barth once suggested that the way to do theology was with the Bible in one hand and the newspaper in the other. This seemed similar: The Bible could guide me only if it was in conversation with real life. Real life was my father, all those years before, reminding me, "The Lord didn't create *anybody* to be under anybody else's boot." My father had once pledged his life to a church whose people would pass a chalice between White and Black mouths without hesitation. We weren't people of exclusion then, and we couldn't be now.

The Episcopal Church is divided into dioceses, which are like districts, democratically governed by an elected bishop. In 2003, when the diocese of New Hampshire elected Rev. Gene Robinson, an openly gay man living with his partner, as its new bishop, I was ready. All the bishops leading dioceses would vote to approve or disapprove his election—and I would vote yes. I knew Bishop

Robinson myself and respected him. But my vote would signal not just my opinion on his election, but my belief that we should amend all our policies to reflect equality for gay and lesbian members.

If the church truly believed that we all are the children of God, and equal before God, then we had to learn how to truly own that and live that. Our commitment to be an inclusive church is not based on a social theory or a cultural trend, but on our belief that the outstretched arms of Jesus on the cross are a sign of the very love of God reaching out to us all. It was time to own that—and yet do it in a way that respected those who saw things differently.

I was growing, and my own beliefs had evolved. But another way to say it is that I was becoming more and more open to letting the spirit of God breathe through me and make me new. Therein is the source of real personal change, evolution, and transformation, and it's never-ending.

WITH BISHOP ROBINSON ELECTED, my head and my heart were working much better together. My stomach settled. And then came the second part of any journey of change: staying the course when the ground starts shaking around you. I wrote a letter to the diocese explaining my position. It caused some rumbles but didn't get too much reaction. However, when a majority of the bishops in the United States voted to consecrate Bishop Robinson in August 2003, the earthquake hit. News of our first openly acknowledged gay bishop made headlines in papers all over the United States and around the world.

The backlash I experienced after the vote was not unique. Many of my fellow bishops and clergy had very similar experiences and struggles. It was a hard time for the church. And yet, good faithful people on all sides of the question have since found a way to live in love, while embracing real differences. But I'm getting to the end of the story.

In that moment, many of us were openly opposed by some of the clergy in our respective states and dioceses. I was bitterly criticized from some pulpits and in local newspaper op-eds in North Carolina. I traveled the diocese to explain my position and the action of the church in town hall–style gatherings, much like those I had held before I was elected. Except now, instead of experiencing a friendly welcome, I was again and again on the receiving end of rage. This continued for two solid years. Keep in mind, the anger I'm talking about was channeled into conversations, speeches, emails, letters, and phone calls. That was very real, but Bishop Robinson, meanwhile, was living in a Kevlar vest. He and his partner were receiving death threats. That's real courage.

In the midst of it all, Rev. Marie Moorefield Fleisher, a senior adviser on our staff, gave me a refrigerator magnet with a picture of John Wayne on it. At first I was perplexed, but then I looked closer and read the quote: "Courage is being scared to death, but saddling up anyway."

Coming from Marie, that meant a lot. Marie was one of the "Philadelphia 11," the first women who were ordained Episcopal priests before church law allowed it. The reaction to women demanding equal treatment by the church in 1974 was similar to what we were seeing now in 2003. Those brave women lived with the anger and pain that are the burden of history's "firsts," those who pave the way of change. Marie and her peers paid a price, and knew firsthand that courage really is being scared to death and saddling up anyway.

After one of our town hall meetings, an elderly Black woman came up to me. She said that during the meeting, she had closed her eyes. She had heard the loud, desperate voices, filled with anger and fear—and she realized she had heard them before. In the 1960s, when she joined the civil rights struggle in Greensboro, she heard it. Here it was again, the very same language and anger that was stirred in the fight against Jim Crow segregation.

Still, I noticed something. While some people were upset and expressing that, the majority were supportive or politely silent. There is very often a sensible center, a silent or quiet majority who are being drowned out by the loudest, most extreme voices. But they are there. Many are simply waiting for the angry to exhaust themselves. They listen patiently, waiting for a deeper wisdom to emerge.

Something else happened with some regularity. Quietly a parent would whisper in my ear, "Thank you." They would tell me that their son or daughter, niece or nephew, was gay. This happened regularly. And when it did, it was a reminder of why working through this painful transition mattered. My challenge was nothing compared with the pain of gays and lesbians, silently endured for decades, even generations. Bishop Robinson's courage, and that of those Christians who stayed with the church even when the church hurt them, is what President John F. Kennedy might have called "profiles in courage." These were people who loved God, followed Jesus, and served in the church, even when the church did not fully welcome them. They believed that the Spirit, with their help, would eventually work to bring about justice. That's faith. That's courage. And a great many of us were committed to honoring it and righting this terrible wrong.

My only challenge was learning how to receive anger and not give it back in return. I needed to do something very difficult: to stand and kneel at the same time. I needed to stand in my conviction, laying out what I believed and why. And when the response was anger, I needed to learn to kneel before it. Believe me, standing in self-righteousness is so much easier. But when you're facing someone else who feels as strongly in their conviction as you do, anger is totally unproductive. Actually it's counterproductive. You've got to create space for the other person.

This is the dance of nonviolent change. You develop

the spiritual discipline of receiving and then letting go, receiving and letting go, receiving then letting go. This isn't easy, and it's even harder if the anger is coming at you from people you love and cherish, rather than strangers. I found it helpful to remember a few things. First, I wasn't God. No one is God. And therefore I was not the ultimate decider of who was right. I could only do what I believed to be right as best I could discern it.

Second, this wasn't about me, ultimately. They weren't angry at me but at what I represented. I found helpful the teaching of Rabbi Edwin Friedman, who was also a family therapist and leadership expert. He talked about how important it was for leaders to be "self-differentiated," knowing where one's self ends and another's begins. If you know your own purpose, you can stay out of the emotional fray your beliefs may stir up in others. If I reacted in anger, I would add even more destructive anxiety to the situation. I knew enough about human nature to know that a sense of safety, not anxiety, is what puts people in a space to open their hearts to change.

Third, I started intentionally praying for the clergy who were speaking against me. I didn't pray for them to change their minds. I prayed for them as children of God. The same love that made space for Michael Curry and Bishop Robinson could make space for them, too. We are all the children of God.

And finally, in the midst of the backlash, a grace note came in the form of a phone conversation with my father's older sister, Aunt Carrie, the last living matriarch of the family. So many years before, after my mother passed, my father had told my sister and me that if anything happened to my father, we'd have a loving home at Aunt Carrie's.

By the time of Bishop Robinson's consecration, Aunt Carrie was eighty years old. She called me one day and said, "Michael, I'm so proud of you. This is the right thing to do." My father and other elders growing up had all passed by that time. My father had once told me before he passed that he had given relationship counseling to two gay members of his church, but I still sometimes wondered what he would think about my position and actions as bishop. That conversation with Aunt Carrie became my family's blessing, a blessing from the ancestors.

In 2004, I gave permission to clergy to bless the unions of gay and lesbian Christians. We provided guidelines for clergy and congregations to support education, conversation, and spiritual reflection as they decided how to proceed. Conscience would always be respected. No member of the clergy and no congregation would be compelled to bless a same-sex union. Each could decide what was appropriate for their community. Meanwhile, there were joyful, moving ceremonies taking place in our churches. Robert and his partner, Lee, were among the first to receive the blessing of their union. Five years later, the two were legally married in New York.

A few years later, when some in North Carolina sought

to amend the state constitution to define legal marriage as only between a man and a woman, I along with many others publicly opposed it. Although the amendment to the constitution did pass, many Episcopalians had fought it. Some because they believed in the equal right to marry. Others because of the belief that the purpose of a constitution is not to take away rights but to enshrine and protect them. But for me, this was a spiritual and moral concern. Loving your neighbor as yourself means recognizing the right of everybody to make a life with the person they love. And it also means making room and space for those who honestly and respectfully hold a different position.

The late Verna Dozier, the English teacher at Dunbar High School in Washington, D.C., who in retirement became one of the finest biblical interpreters of The Episcopal Church, was a real mentor, teacher, and soul friend to me. In her book *The Dream of God*, she offered this wisdom: "We always see through a glass darkly, and that is what faith is about. I will live by the best I can discern today. Tomorrow I may find out I was wrong. Since I do not live by being right, I am not destroyed by being wrong."

CHAPTER 9

The Real E Pluribus Unum

Question: Do I have to love even my enemy?

The door to the mind should only open from the heart.
An enemy who gets in, risks the danger
of becoming a friend.
—U.S. POET LAUREATE JOY HARJO,
"THIS MORNING I PRAY FOR MY ENEMIES"

WHEN I WAS bishop of North Carolina, a reporter asked me what the biggest challenge facing the church was. I answered him, "We're wrestling with sexuality now, we know that. But I think the greater challenge is this: How do we make e pluribus unum—out of many, one—real, without obliterating anybody?"

That's not just the church's challenge. It is our nation's challenge. It is the world's challenge. How do we walk together as brothers and sisters, united by some ancient and venerated values and hopes, when we also have significant difference and disagreement?

We need e pluribus unum now more than ever—because if we don't work together, we'll likely work against all our interests. The large-scale problems we face as humans will not be solved by isolation. When we're busy wagging fingers at each other, we can't move away from the nightmare and closer to the dream. The planet is suffering, and if we don't heal her, we're about to feel the blunt impact—some more than others, but eventually, all of us. We're all in this together.

There's a very real parallel in The Episcopal Church. We spent thirty years fighting the culture wars, thankfully with the positive outcome of a church that looks more like love. In 2015, twelve years after Bishop Robinson's consecration in New Hampshire, we changed the marriage canon to be gender neutral. Marriage in the church today is the loving union of two of God's divine creatures. We don't use the language of "gay and lesbian issues" anymore; we say, "issues of human sexuality." This isn't about "those people" and "their issues." This is about being people and being a church that recognizes and welcomes the beautiful tapestry of humankind.

On June 26, 2015, the Supreme Court in *Obergefell v. Hodges* ruled that state bans on same-sex marriage were illegal. The right to marry was guaranteed for all. And on June 27, I was elected presiding bishop of The Episcopal Church, this time on the first ballot.

The enthusiasm that elected me wasn't so much about me, Michael Curry. If anything, I gave voice to a widely felt sense that it was time to refocus ourselves as Episcopalians on work that would make a difference not primarily for the church, but for our society and global community.

Less than two weeks before my election, a lone White supremacist had killed nine African Americans at Charleston's Mother Emanuel Church, the oldest African Methodist Episcopal church in the South. They had invited him in for Bible study and a prayer meeting.

And later that year, delegates from 196 countries signed the Paris Agreement, a framework for international cooperation on actions to mitigate greenhouse gas emissions and address climate change.

These events would help shape my new office's priorities, which we summarized as *evangelism, racial reconciliation*, and *care of God's creation. Evangelism* is a word with a lot of baggage that to me simply means modeling Jesus's love in our daily lives and finding opportunities as a church to share that love. *Racial reconciliation* means healing the wounds that divide and separate us as children of God. And *care of God's creation* means helping to heal the planet from destruction and harm. These were all one with the foundational mission of the church: to follow the way of Jesus and his love to foster a loving, liberating, and life-giving relationship with God, with each other as children of God, and indeed with all God's creation. Therein is the work of building God's beloved community. That's e pluribus unum for real.

It may be time we do something similar as citizens of this democracy, to move past our differences and step together into hope. Together is the only way to face the challenges ahead. We need to find a way to *unum* even when we know that we the people are beautifully, confoundingly *pluribus*. We need to leave behind contempt. Contempt is the belief that the person who disagrees with you isn't just wrong, but worthless. It's a killer when it comes to marriages, they've found, and it's no better for any other human relationship. Try making meaningful progress when contempt controls the discussion. It's like trying to grow plants in radioactive soil.

My election signaled our eagerness as a church to move past our internal disputes. The same convention that had elected me had also voted to change the church law governing marriage. The reform passed relatively easily, signaling how much progress we had made stateside, despite a wide range of attitudes toward sexuality. The reaction outside the United States was something else. It unfortunately sparked a new global phase of the culture war. The Anglican Communion, which represents more than 85 million people around the world, exploded in reaction. Simply put, the rest of the Anglican world—in particular, churches in many African countries, where more than half the world's Anglicans live—were not ready to accept gay marriage.

The archbishop of Canterbury in England—the spiritual head of the communion—summoned the more than thirty primary leaders (called primates) from the church's provinces around the world together for a meeting. The idea was we'd all sit in a room and deal with our differences about marriage. The date of the meeting was delayed until after my consecration, possibly in hopes that the same need for fresh air and forward movement that got me elected would oxygenate the world stage. And so, one of my first big tasks in my new role was to travel to Canterbury to sit in a room, once again, to talk about human sexuality and who deserved our welcome as a church. There were those among my brother primates who wanted The Episcopal Church—a.k.a. TEC—suspended from the communion. I went with real hope that somehow I could change their minds, or at the very least help promote some better understanding of what we had done and why.

The Stakes of Fracture

On the long flight from New York to London, I had plenty of time to think about the stakes. The possibility of schism was deeply unsettling. To my mind, the very integrity of the church was at issue. If we, the followers of Jesus of Nazareth, of the God who is love, could not find a way to live together in peace, even when members were in real disagreement, who could? One of the most important functions of the Church is to be a sanctuary in which people can disagree, even vehemently, and yet still see the other as a brother or sister in Christ. If we cannot do this ourselves, then we have no ground to preach unity and reconciliation to others. There's no such thing as a perfect institution. The Episcopal Church, like the United States, has many sins in its past—ugly legacies of colonialism, anti-Semitism, racism, and sexism. Many people are now reckoning with that past, and doing the hard work of reconciliation and healing.

But, again like the United States, the Anglican Communion does real good, on a huge scale, at home and in the world. If the communion were to break apart, whether because of America's "rogue behavior" or because of its own internal disagreements, the result would be real harm to our brothers and sisters living in circumstances that require the church's support and protection.

The worldwide Anglican community is one of the largest humanitarian service delivery systems in the world. Anglican churches, alongside other faith communities, have a reach that governments and other organizations often don't have. We are just about everywhere. In many places in the developing world, particularly in Africa, the network of churches and their leaders, from parish priests to archbishops, has weathered everything from coup d'états to dictatorships. In 2005, I was in downtown Burundi, where a decade of civil war had resulted in hundreds of thousands of deaths. I stood outside the building in which the diocese had its offices. It was surrounded by blocks and blocks of rubble, a city and its people gutted by bloody war. On the top of the building was its name, Peace House, a symbol of hope that the nightmare could someday be transformed. Where everything else had been destroyed, that building remained.

Again, it's not just hope and symbolism we're talking about. The stakes are utterly concrete. Amid political turbulence, local churches provide stable practical infrastructure for humanitarian relief. They provide education. In Haiti, for example, The Episcopal Church is the largest educator on the island. Any fracturing of the support system could interrupt the delivery of services in schools, hospitals, food distribution centers, and missions. It's not an overstatement to say that if the communion were to split, people relying on our services could die.

Walking off the plane in London, I experienced more than the usual sense of discombobulation after an international flight. There was a simple reason: Six weeks earlier, I'd had brain surgery. That's right. The day of my installation as presiding bishop, I had tripped on a curb while getting coffee near the National Cathedral in Washington, D.C. I didn't know it, but the bump on my head had created a slow internal bleed. I was preaching in Bruton Parish Church in Williamsburg, Virginia, about six weeks later when the damage finally presented itself. From the pulpit, I was speaking gibberish, frequently saying the opposite of what I intended to communicate. The crowd, kind Episcopalians all, sat politely through my nonsense, but afterward, the Reverend Michael Hunn, a member of our staff who was with me, and a doctor in the congregation who had grown more and more concerned as she listened, gently guided me to a room. The doctor, Kate Roberts, took a look at me and decided that I needed to get to a hospital. Just a few hours later, I was being prepped for surgery. It was a literal head trip. I was too confused and shocked to be frightened. I told my surgeon, "I need to be in Canterbury in January." He turned out to be Episcopalian, and said, "I'm going to make sure I get you well enough to get to that meeting and keep us in the communion, Bishop Curry."

In the months that followed, I went to rehab several times a week. As a sixty-plus-year-old man, I had the humbling experience of learning to read and write for the second time in my life. When I received my little gold-stamped certificate of completion, I felt like a proud first grader getting his first Good Citizenship Award. And yet, I wasn't completely recovered. My concentration was at maybe 50 percent capacity. Meanwhile I had a new tool-kit of cognitive hacks to keep me focused and on track. (Some of them I still find useful, like jotting down key-words when someone is speaking.)

At Heathrow Airport that day, my true vulnerability became clear. My brain was completely overwhelmed by stimuli, despite all that I had learned in occupational therapy—tricks like walking right next to the wall so that you're out of the main flow of traffic. Fortunately I was with Sharon Jones and Chuck Robertson, members of our staff. I couldn't have done it by myself. Decisions I nor-mally made without any conscious thought were instead big, deliberative moments. So many people, so much data, so much noise, so many choices to make. I would read a sign and then forget what it said before I could act on the information.

I had a moment of panic; could I do this meeting? Later that night I would pray in my dormitory bed that the Spirit would carry me through the days ahead. It helped that I had years of experience in the task ahead of me, having worked so long to keep the church together in North Carolina. The fallout there after Bishop Robinson's election, and throughout the next decade, had been more than angry parishioners. There had been lawsuits, and a few dioceses threatened to leave the church. I thought back to the "Covenant of Respectful Conversation" that we had shared before gatherings in the months and years after. It had four principles:

1. Listen to each other.
2. Pray for each other.
3. Love each other.
4. Discern together to hear what the Spirit might be saying to the Church.

There were primates in the communion who were offended by what we had done. But there were multiple levels to their reaction. True, they had strikingly different attitudes toward human sexuality. But they were also resentful. The Anglican Communion is the third-largest Christian

body in the world, behind the Roman Catholic and Ortho-
dox traditions. For some, this was an experience of imperi-
alism all over again: the Americans foisting their power
and culture on the rest of the world, without regard for local traditions. From their point of view, we had no right to
change the marriage canons unilaterally; any change of
doctrine, the official teachings, should be a decision of the
worldwide communion, not just one branch. Our decisions
and actions reopened real wounds, and I understood that.
There were primates whose bishops and clergy were count-
ing on them to come home having won a victory.

It was entirely possible that the church might fracture
or split. It was that serious.

Maybe it was good that my brain was operating at 50
percent. It made it easier to hear my heart. And my heart
told me that despite all these differences, we could find a
way to walk together. We had to. Still, back at the airport,
I held tight to my colleague's arm until we got into a car
for the ninety-mile drive to Kent, the home of Canterbury Cathedral.

One Body Under Christ

It's hard not to be impressed by Canterbury Cathedral. It is
the mother church of Anglican Christianity. The current
structure was built in 1077, but people have been gathering
there daily to pray since 597. Even I can do the math: That's
more than 1,400 years, or seven times older than the

United States. That's a lot of people and a lot of prayers. Its dramatic Gothic spires tower over the narrow stone streets of Canterbury. More than a hundred archbishops have presided there, all the way back to St. Augustine, sent there in the sixth century by Pope Gregory the Great.

During the weeklong conference, the cathedral grounds were cloistered from the press, as they always are when the primates meet. This is important. Shutting reporters out creates space for free discussion, without the pressure of imagining your words as tomorrow's headline. And being in that quiet, cordoned-off world, at one of the world's most enduring destinations for spiritual pilgrimage, helps everyone show up and be present as individuals.

Every day, we met in the cathedral for morning prayers, then went down the steps into the crypt for Communion. Then we'd move to the conference center for working sessions, which were hours of discussion and debate, broken up by tea and more prayers. Looming over us in the crypt each morning was Pope Gregory's crozier, which had been sent from Rome by Pope Francis to be present at our meetings. It was a symbol of support, a reminder that we weren't alone. But there was another message, too: The community of this church has an ancient lineage; don't forget it. Later in the week, they had the book of Gospels delivered in a glass box to be present during our closing service. That's the book that the archbishops of Canterbury, all the way back to Augustine, have used to take their oath of office.

Early in the week, while most were gracious, polite

and friendly, there were two or three people who wouldn't speak to me. When I said "hello," they acknowledged me civilly but did what they could to avoid direct contact or conversation. Lunches were quiet, and they didn't sit with me. Throughout, I practiced that same skill honed in North Carolina. I stood and kneeled at once. I kept myself grounded in an attitude of positivity and hope. At the end of each day, I didn't know whether my behavior made a difference. I only knew that I felt comfortable with what I had contributed.

WHEN IT CAME to possible outcomes, there were two extremes. The communion could do nothing, simply accepting that Americans would have a different interpretation of the marriage canon. Or, as some of the conservative primates, primarily from Africa, probably arrived hoping to do, we could be suspended from the communion completely—a position that primates from the more liberal countries would not accept.

Our discussions were frank and difficult, but respectful. Still, it was hard. Thousands of years of religious traditions, commonly held by most of humanity, were being challenged. For some, the very faith itself was being challenged. The tension was real. The future of the third-largest Christian body in the world was uncertain. The future of gay and lesbian Christians in the church was being determined, without any of them in the room.

The archbishop, after a few days of heated discussion, introduced an informal vote. By a show of hands, would we agree to walk together in Christ, even though there might be distance between us? I knew that this vote, while informal, would be a deciding moment. If we had enough people to commit to walking together, as one body of Christ, we could come to some resolution that would keep the church together. I looked around, watching my fellow primates. Hands went up around the room. As the passage in the New Testament says, it seemed we would "walk in love, as Christ loved us and gave himself for us."[1] It was a moment of commitment made possible by our shared faith and long-standing relationships, and a godly love that transcended any division. But we weren't out of the woods yet.

The next day or so, we all participated in a foot-washing ceremony. The tradition comes from the Bible, when Jesus washes his disciples' feet. At first they demure, but Jesus essentially says, "This way of humility, this way of love, is my way. You have a choice, get washed or get going." When he's finished, he tells them to wash each other's feet, too. The point is clear, but he says it anyway: "Very truly I tell you, no servant is greater than his master, nor is a messenger greater than the one who sent him."

I invite you to imagine this: Grown men dressed in purple, washing each other's feet in plastic basins, walking barefoot across the floor of a thousand-year-old crypt, in all its gritty glory. If you've ever done it, you know it's a little awkward, and comforting. I don't know what it is about feet, but exposing them and letting another person wash them is disorienting. You're not in control. I've found it harder to have my feet washed than to wash the feet of another. This is humans meeting each other's humanity in a very visceral way. Our bare skin, our smells, our vulnerability. This is people being humble with each other, and real with each other. I couldn't tell you who washed whose feet that day, only that no one refused.

From that point on, we were moving gradually toward resolution. The rest of the debate was about what walking together in love, despite our differences, looked like in practice. There were many hours of hard conversations, but they were productive. It was eventually decided that for a period of three years, we in The Episcopal Church would have to live with some consequences of our decisions and actions. During that time, because we had deviated from the doctrine and teaching of Anglican Christianity, no representatives of TEC (a.k.a. the Americans) would be allowed to represent the Anglican Communion in ecumenical and interfaith dialogues. Nothing would change in our relationship with the communion except that. In practical terms, the impact was minimal, with only a few of our TEC representatives directly affected. It could have been far worse.

Afterward, everyone would go home and catch flak from those in their constituencies who might have wanted either more extreme or more lenient measures—including me. Before the news could hit, I went outside with Chuck Robertson, my canon for external relations, who, with Matthew Davies of our communications staff, filmed an iPhone video of me explaining the decision the primates had come to.

It was January, and a cold wind was blowing so hard I had to hold down my winter hat. I tried not to shiver as I prepared to speak through the camera to my fellow Episcopalians back home. But again, I found myself struggling to find the right words. I asked Chuck and Matt for help, and they coached me through. Between their help, and the thought of all the people back home praying for everyone gathered at Canterbury that week, the words came.

I shared that the decision represented the consequences of our action as a church. We had not changed the vow of marriage, but we had expanded who could be married, in line with our belief that gay and lesbian followers of Jesus deserved equality within the church. Doing so was not unlike an act of civil disobedience in which one violates an unjust law both to change the law and, more importantly, to prick the conscience, awakening the heart to the universal human cry. The prick may not yield immediate resolution, but it creates room and space for relationships that in time find a way forward honoring the dignity of all.

Internally I was able to be at some peace. We had not reached a complete solution to our differences in the communion, but we had identified a spiritual way together.

LOVE MAKES IT possible to disagree on bedrock convictions and yet stay in a relationship. There is a valid concern that doing so forces you to compromise on principles. But sometimes you have to run the risk because of a greater danger: chaos and social self-destruction. I think we have to run that risk, especially in the church. We have to know that love can survive meaningful disagreements. The union can endure, and must endure. Likewise, in our nation, if we can't make room for people with differing viewpoints, we aren't living in a democracy anymore. We're in a dictatorship.

The primates' sanction was a compromise, but a healthy one. Lots of folks worked hard that week to get there, though not everybody made it. For the great majority, we walked together, while those who needed it found a formal way to express disagreement with the American wing of the church. The disagreement was real, but we were clear: You don't divide the body of Christ. We would walk together as family.

I mentioned the quiet lunches early in the week at Canterbury. As the week progressed, and we had been together 24/7, getting barefoot together, working toward a place where we could stand with integrity, lunchtime conversation loosened up. By the last lunches, some of the people who at first wouldn't sit with me were now making conversation. And I noticed something. The more personal we became with each other, the more people's animosity seemed to fall away. We couldn't demonize each other when we knew each other well, one reason that debates with strangers on social media—or even between friends but in the disassociated space of email or text—escalate so quickly and are often unproductive.

As we opened up over meals, some spoke personally about climate change, from the Pacific Rim to Africa's Mount Kilimanjaro. It struck me then that all that week while we were enumerating and debating our disagreements, urgent life or death issues were going unheard. It struck me then more powerfully than ever: We have to move past our differences to work together on ways we can make things better. We can't sit in rooms arguing. We can't waste our energy on hate or unproductive opposition.

I thought a lot that week about what words I could offer after the vote to influence relationships positively going forward. The night before the vote and final meeting day, I sat there with my blank tablet. My brain, exhausted and battered, was fighting for words and concentration. But my heart, or the spirit working through me, knew what it wanted to say.

I wrote words that I was afraid were too honest, too personal. I was afraid I wouldn't be able to effectively deliver them. But I wrote them anyway. I needed to say something that could create the context for long-term healing—not just in the communion, but in the gay and

lesbian community that had been hurt by the church for
so long. We had hammered out a way forward, but something more was needed.

Just prior to the formal censure vote being cast on the
final day, I hit pause on my panic button and delivered
the speech I had prepared.

Your Graces,

The resolution before us will be painful for many in
The Episcopal Church to receive.

Many of us have committed ourselves and our church
to being "a house of prayer for all people," as the Bible
says, where all are truly welcome. Our commitment to
be an inclusive church is not based on a social theory
or capitulation to the ways of the culture, but on our
belief that the outstretched arms of Jesus on the cross
are a sign of the very love of God reaching out to us all.
While I understand that many disagree with us, our decision regarding marriage is based on the belief that
the words of the Apostle Paul to the Galatians are true
for the church today: *"All who have been baptized into
Christ have clothed yourself with Christ. There is no longer Jew or Gentile, slave or free, male or female, for all
are one in Christ."*[2]

But I must say to you in all love and honesty that for
so many who are committed to following Jesus in the
way of love and being a church that lives that love, this
decision will bring real pain.

For fellow disciples of Jesus in our church who are gay or lesbian, this will bring more pain. For many who have felt and been rejected by the church because of who they are, for many who have felt and been rejected by families and communities, our church opening itself in love was a sign of hope. And this will add pain on top of pain.

And while I in no sense compare my own pain to theirs I stand before you as your brother. I stand before you as a descendant of African slaves, stolen from their native land, enslaved in a bitter bondage, and then even after emancipation, segregated and excluded in church and society. And this conjures that up again, and brings pain.

The pain for many will be real. But God is greater than anything. I love Jesus and I love the church. I am a Christian in the Anglican way. And like you, as we have said in this meeting, I am committed to "walking together" with you as fellow primates in the Anglican family.

I love you, for you are my brothers and I am your brother in Jesus Christ. And regardless of the outcome of this vote, we shall continue to walk together in that love.

That statement was the first thing of any length that I had written since the surgery, and I was far from fully healed. There is no doubt in my mind that the prayers of many people summoned those words into being. I couldn't have written it or read it on my own. Prayer isn't a magical granting of wishes, but it does change things. Summoned by prayers, the Spirit moved through me that day. I'd experienced it before, but never so powerfully.

I had one other powerful realization as we wrapped up the week. We had all arrived at Canterbury knowing that we might fail. It was a very real possibility. Our attempts to resolve conflict could have resulted in hurt and harm to the communion and everyone it touches. And yet we all took the risk and accepted the potential of sacrifice. We did so because of a simple truth: Failure to love is guaranteed to fail. We had to meet in love, and make whatever baby steps we could, because refusing to do so—backing away from the challenge—would have eclipsed even the possibility of a shared future.

Praying with Your Feet

A few years later, the night before I would let the Spirit lead me once more, through my preaching at the royal wedding, I found myself sitting next to the archbishop of Canterbury taking questions from a journalist. One reporter said, "We know that the two of you disagree on same-sex marriage. So how is it that the two of you are sitting here together and will be together at this wedding tomorrow?" We both gave very similar answers. I said something like, "This is my brother, we follow Jesus. He teaches us the way of love; he didn't teach us the way of agreement. That love dominates our relationship, not our agreements or disagreements."

When Jesus talked about love, he was talking about a commitment and a way of life. Emotions come and go. But when Jesus of Nazareth tells the parable of the Good Samaritan, the love he's demonstrating is a determination and commitment to do what is best and right and good, as well as you can figure it out, for the other. Jesus didn't say "like your enemies." Because you don't have to like them—you only have to love them. You've got to keep your commitment to seek the common good, and figure out what "good" looks like for each relationship, even the ones with people you'd rather not have over for dinner.

In the United States and in the world, we have different cultures, different politics, different experiences that have shaped our beliefs. But if we can establish that we're working toward some common good, whether we like each other or not, then we can be brothers and sisters even when we want to fight like hell. Let's all stop worrying about whether we like each other and choose to believe instead that we're capable of doing good together. That doesn't solve all our problems, not by far, but it at least gets us in the starting gate. It gets us unstuck. It's how human beings can live together in profound difference. It's the start of an e pluribus unum that's safe for everybody.

Later in 2016, when Donald Trump was elected, the Washington National Cathedral prepared to host the

Inaugural Prayer Service, a nonpartisan practice that goes back decades. But this time, there were many good folk who seriously questioned whether the service should be held. My answer was a resounding yes. During the election, we had learned things about the president-elect that created great concern and worry. To pray for him could bring pain to many.

And yet if love is your purpose, that was exactly the time to pray, for the president and the nation. It was and still is the time to double down on prayer. Because prayer, real prayer, is both contemplative and active. Quietly, we pray for the president. But then there's the active side of prayer, as we live the truth of "love your neighbor as yourself." Part of that is working for a good, just, humane, and loving society. That means getting on our knees for the president, and it *also* means standing on our feet and marching in the streets. It means praying through participation in the life of our government and society. Through caring for others. Through working for policies and laws that reflect Jesus's call to love your neighbor, to do unto others as you would have them do unto you. Through fashioning a civic order that reflects goodness, justice, and compassion, and the very heart and dream of God for all of God's children and God's creation.

To love, my brothers and sisters, does not mean we have to agree. But maybe agreeing to love is the greatest agreement. And the only one that ultimately matters, because it makes a future possible.

CHAPTER 10

The Great Relationship Revival

Question: How can love overcome what divides us and move us forward together?

> *Let us put our minds together and see what life we can make for our children.*
> —CHIEF SITTING BULL

ON MARCH 10, 2016, then–presidential candidate Donald Trump spoke at a campaign rally in Fayetteville, North Carolina. The rally was disrupted by protesters, as happened around the country at both Trump and Clinton rallies. Eventually law enforcement officials led the protesters out. As they did, a seventy-nine-year-old Trump supporter named John McGraw, who is White, jumped out from the crowd and punched one of the detained protesters, Rakeem Jones, in the face. Jones is Black. Afterward, McGraw said on video, "He deserved it . . . The next time we see him we might have to kill him . . . We don't know who he is. He might be with a terrorist organization."

Notice the language: *We don't know who he is.* That is profoundly telling.

McGraw was arrested and charged with assault. Months later the two men met again in court, where McGraw pleaded no contest, apologized, and was sentenced to twelve months of probation. Afterward, they faced each other and shook hands. McGraw said, "If I met you in the street and the same thing occurred, I would have said, 'Go on home. One of us will get hurt. That's what I would have said. But we are caught up in a political mess today, and you and me, we got to heal our country."[1] Later, at Jones's request, they had lunch together.

That encounter, though physical and blunt, is emblematic of the divisions that are rocking our country. Abraham Lincoln, quoting the words of Jesus, was right when he said that "a house divided against itself cannot stand." And if the truth be told, in many places in the world, not just the United States, love for one's country is degenerating into calls to exclude and evict our neighbors.

Here in the United States, we have to find a way to *unum* if we're going to contribute to a safe, healthy, loving world for our children and their children. And yet the divisions are there, and they are many.

They are racial. Racism today is dangerous and real for millions of Americans. Yet plenty of good people hold tight to the belief that American society is color-blind, because to believe otherwise is far too painful. Their ignorance, in turn, causes great pain.

They are socioeconomic. There are people in this country who have benefited from the gifts of wealth, opportunity, and education, and those who feel they have not.

They are political. Words like "human scum," "losers," and "criminals" have replaced an honest civil discourse. Both sides of the political spectrum have been overtaken by anger.

For all those who feel unheard, ignored, and under siege, these divisions are particularly painful and real. Powerful forces exploit that pain, and here we are: Wrought by extremism. Mistrustful. Punching each other in the face, in so many ways. And above all, doubting our shared future. That's one thing that we can all be sure of: Whatever the future holds, it will be shared. We'll live together as family or perish as fools.

But God is not finished with us yet. Love has not left this land. There are many among us who are ready to move forward with one voice that says, *No more. We choose love! We choose community!* But to get there, we have work to do. We need to heal. Without healing, claims to unity feel disingenuous. We can't work together, or get to know each other, if we don't trust each other. When McGraw and Jones shook hands, plenty of people shook their heads, uneasy. It wasn't just the punch that became emblematic, it was the televised handshake that newscasters spun as instant healing. We need healing stories—but they need to be authentic, which takes time.

To move two steps forward, we all need to slow down

and take one step back. As post-apartheid South Africa showed us, truth comes before reconciliation. It's time to tell each other the truth, and to listen to each other's truth. Stories are how we do that. They're the beginning of a relationship revival.

It's time that we each take a close look at how we can contribute. Sharing stories is a powerful opportunity, but it requires us all to step outside our comfort zones. That stepping out is emotional, but it's also literal. Many of us live inside bubbles, whether we mean to or not. It's time to step out and, in listening to each other, to write a new story.

MY EXPERIENCE WITH the Sioux at Standing Rock has been my most life-changing experience of stepping out and seeing what happens when good people seek to change the story. My time in North Dakota fundamentally re-shaped my understanding of the world and my place in it.

The story began for me in 2016 when I received a letter from Bishop Michael Smith, Father John Floberg, and the council of the Episcopal Church in North Dakota. In the letter, they asked if I would make a pastoral visit to the Sioux Standing Rock Reservation, where an oil pipeline was being built just south of its border. Its planned route was through sacred burial grounds and would cross under the Missouri River at Lake Oahe, endangering the water supply for the eight thousand people living on the reservation. They needed help to make the struggle there more visible.

At that point, I didn't know much about the pipeline. The situation had just started to attract some attention from environmentalists and social justice activists, but most mainline churches, like most Americans, didn't know what was going on. Floberg and others were calling, but not many were answering.

I didn't then know much about the Episcopalians on the reservation or about the life of the people there. The stories of Indigenous people in our country, forced onto reservations, are often hidden and unknown. Ralph Ellison's powerful image of the experience of disinherited, disenfranchised peoples as "the invisible man" remains a haunting truth.

From John Floberg and other teachers, I learned the history of my own church's involvement with the Sioux. In cooperation with the U.S. government after the Civil War, the church became the spiritual and tactical frontline in the forced assimilation of Native Americans on the reservations.

Historically, the church's disregard for the rights and autonomy of Indigenous people went back much, much further, to the Pope's Doctrine of Discovery in the fifteenth century, which basically gave Portugal the church's blessing to conquer and enslave anyone who wasn't Christian. And so, still today, we have a world that looks nothing like the God who the Bible says is love.

Now the Standing Rock Sioux were again under siege, and they were gathering in defense of their land. They wanted and needed all the support they could get, leading to our clergy raising the call. John Floberg saw an opportunity for the church to show up for the Sioux in a completely different way—in support and witness, serving them and responding to their need. It was a chance for healing, with the realization that our support now, if welcomed, could make a real difference. But so far, John had not had much luck getting people's attention. When he came to me, I was more than willing to go. These were Episcopalians who had been largely invisible to me. If they were calling, I was coming. They weren't going to be invisible anymore.

Water Is Life

At first, I saw my trip to Standing Rock primarily as being about racial justice. I mentioned earlier the three priorities that had gotten me elected as presiding bishop. We had started with two, evangelism and racial reconciliation. But the third pillar, care of God's creation, I added at the urging of my team. Until then, I had never seen environmentalism as a core issue. I recycled my cans and was anxious about climate change, like everyone else, but I didn't consider it a spiritual concern. It was an issue for politicians and planners, not priests. Nevertheless, we added care of creation as an official pillar of my office because wise people told me I needed to get with it.

I arrived in North Dakota in September of that year, unprepared for the effect that the land and people would have on me. I was born and raised in the urban density of the East. The endless brown plains and open skies immediately reoriented my understanding of our place in the world. We human beings are so small, so very dependent on the rhythms of the earth, which we do not control and yet have thrown off-kilter. Indigenous people are still bound to the earth in a way we in industrialized areas have forgotten. We city folk are bound to the earth, too, it's just harder to see—though with the effects of climate change, it's getting clearer.

The Oceti Sakowin Camp was on the Cannonball River, adjacent to the pipeline site. This humble hub of teepees and cars represented something historic. Here, the Lakota, Dakota, and Nakota Sioux were coming together as one people for the first time in a hundred years, called by the spirit to protect the water. A sacred flame in the center of camp would mark this reunion, burning without interruption until the group disbanded.

The Sioux were adamant that they were not there as protesters. They were there as water protectors. They were guardians of creation, not agitators. Like all those who have inched the world closer to the dream, they were fighting evil with love rather than with hate.

Everywhere we went, we saw signs: MNÍ WIČÓNI. WA-TER IS LIFE. Coming to understand the struggle of these people led me to a realization: Racial reconciliation and care of creation aren't distinct at all. They are part of the same issue. The very people we have made invisible—ripped from their land, marginalized, and impoverished—are the people who are now shouldering the worst of our environmental harms. It's not just the Indigenous. It is communities of color and the poorest of Americans. Just think about Flint, Michigan, where the municipal water supply became toxic to humans, and to humanity. We can't reconcile with each other without healing our relationship with the one planet that supports us all.

In the Christian faith, water is at the center of one of our most important rituals, baptism. In water, we are given new life in Christ. But it took the Sioux to remind me: Water *is* life. And though no human is more deserving of it than any other, that's not what the world looks like. When I spoke that day at the camp, I told them what I now understood: "Your struggle is not just your struggle; it is our struggle. It is the struggle of the human community." I hoped that this moment would awaken the world to this truth in the way that Selma had awakened the world so many years ago to the evils of segregation.

I left Standing Rock with a new grasp on the work ahead, and the role of the church in protecting creation. We pushed out the story of the Standing Rock water protectors with every tool we had—our news service, our social media, and our network of clergy. And when, a month or so later, John Floberg put out a new call for clergy to come support the tribes, our people flocked. More than five hundred leaders from twenty faith traditions traveled to Standing Rock in November 2016. Stephanie Spellers, our canon who leads our environmental stewardship, was one of them. She is the source of the description of those days that you're about to read.

When those Christian clergy gathered at Standing Rock, they had come to be part of a new story, living in a new relationship with the earth and with Indigenous people. But they did not come to write the story; that was up to the Sioux. And first, there was a very old story, the history I related earlier, which needed to be heard and reckoned with.

On the first night clergy arrived, the Sioux leaders called them together in a gymnasium. The leaders made it clear that they were guests in their land and needed to follow the rules—for one, not to engage in behavior that would get them arrested. You getting arrested doesn't help us, they said. Don't make this about you. Then they told stories. One elder spoke of the earth and the water as grandparents, not resources for exploitation. According to Stephanie, it was almost like this elder was giving the group a primer on how to be in a different kind of relationship with the world. In so much of Western life,

Christian life even, the earth is depicted as an instrument for our use—an object. Now they were awakening to the mutuality of the relationship.

Later, another elder stood at the center and gazed around the room, saying, "We needed you before and you didn't come. But you came now. Thank you." They also thanked the other Indigenous tribes that had reunited at Standing Rock after many years of separation.

The next morning started with a ritual. Standing in the cold November air, elders from each of the major faith traditions present repudiated the ancient Doctrine of Discovery and then burned a copy of it. They then read an apology to Native Americans and to the earth. Though they did not use this language, they apologized for treating creation and the native people as an *It* rather than a *Thou.* For seeing Native Americans as obstacles and objects instead of as fellow creatures of God's great earth, deserving of autonomy and respect. The clergy gathered bowed in sorrow. Stephanie, her voice still full of reverence even years later, told me that it felt like a reckoning, a moment in which each person present took responsibility for what their traditions had contributed to the wounding of the land and the nations.

Does burning a piece of paper solve everything? No. Does apologizing solve everything? No. But it is a necessary step toward a new phase in the relationship. None of the people there personally had anything to do with the doctrine. And yet they were living in and benefiting from the reality the doctrine had created. To move forward, the past needed to be acknowledged, the pain shared.

Then they marched. The Episcopal community of Standing Rock carried a cross at the front of the procession. There was a drumbeat and the shaking of bells as hundreds proceeded from the camp to the pipeline construction site. There, just short of the barriers, they joined hands in a giant circle along the rolling hill of the plain. This was a Niobrara Circle of Life, a tradition the Sioux brought to their churches, where the circle undulates in on itself, giving everyone the opportunity to hug everyone else in the circle without it breaking. Stephanie's exact words capture it best: "There was so much power in being together like that. Feeling like we are knit together. Out under that massive sky on this rolling plain: We are knit together as people. We are knit together as creation. No one who was there could ever forget it."

Stephanie, who is Black, told the entire group gathered part of her own story that day. Growing up, she knew that her people came from the mountains of Appalachia. She also knew that her great-grandmother had jet-black straight hair. She had heard people say "Blackfoot Indian," but no one really knew her grandmother's origins. No one talked about it or told those stories. "What had come clear for me, with everyone gathered on that plain, was that somewhere in our story of becoming American, most of us had been separated from the land and from our stories of being people of the land. People who were enslaved were ripped from their lands. For a lot of us, going to Standing Rock was like coming home to the land again."

The Truth Force

Our stories have power. They have the power to change how people understand the world—but even before that, they have the power to heal the storyteller. It's not easy to tell a painful story. At first, it feels like reliving the trauma. You feel vulnerable in sharing it; sometimes you really are vulnerable when you are telling a truth that people aren't ready to hear. And yet it gives you power. Telling the story, over time, gives you ownership over the experience, and then distances you from it. This is an approach psychologists have used successfully to help people recover from the worst kinds of trauma. Instead of being alone with your story, you're now sharing the burden with all who listen. You are no longer alone.

Stories build bridges between people. Earlier I told you the story in Exodus of Moses and the burning bush. Moses heard the voice of God, saying, "Take off your shoes, for you're standing on sacred ground." An old friend of mine once preached on that text, saying that the reason Moses had to take off his shoes was not that the dirt itself was holy, but that the space was made holy because God was about to tell his story. Whenever someone tells their story, you are standing on holy ground. You behave differently, hear them differently, and react from a different place. It's so much harder to hate when someone has shown you their heart.

I've come to see the sharing of stories as a powerful form of Gandhi's nonviolent action satyagraha, the "truth force." It's standing by and speaking our truth. It's standing and kneeling at the same time. It's protecting not protesting. Stories are not a concession, but the context for conversion of the heart.

There is power here. Whether the tales of Zen masters, old rabbis, or Methodist circuit riders carrying the story into unknown frontiers, the classic religious imagination has long known that there is something in our stories. To put it in "preacher-speak," the language I know best, stories are the song of the soul sung in the language of life. That's why the hearing and telling of our stories has the power and the capacity to move us to deeper levels of our selves. It was Shakespeare in *Richard II* who placed on the lips of one of his characters the words "let us sit upon the ground and tell sad stories of the death of kings."

Stories allow for the communion of spirits. I can't commune with your spirit without in some sense being changed by it. You can't commune with my spirit without in some sense being changed by it. Our stories are the song of the soul sung in the language of life.

THE STANDING ROCK story did not have a happy ending. What seemed to be a victory under one presidential administration in September 2016, when construction was temporarily halted, gave way to a reversal under the new one. In 2017, the pipeline was completed.

Early that year, the Sioux had made the decision to extinguish the sacred fire that had burned in the camp's center and close the camp down. The land needed to be cleaned of debris before the spring thaw, when the area would become a flood plain. But in truth, the story isn't over. After closing the camp, they released this statement:

> The sacred fire of the Seven Councils has been put to sleep.
> The sacred fire can be lit in our hearts internally and spiritually forever.
> The Horn has been filled with water and love, and now the seeds of this water and love are being given to the world . . .

The Sioux gave us that hopeful segue. *"The seeds of this water and love are being given to the world."* That battle was lost, but seeds of love were spread and sown. The seeds of a new story had been born: of reclaimed unity within the tribes, in North America and around the world. There was a realization that people of good will, of all religions, stripes, and types, can come together for good. For so many people around the world, Standing Rock was a defining moment when consciousness and awareness of the sacredness of our world and climate rose dramatically.

Your Daily Truth Force

Now to be honest, Standing Rock may seem remote from your daily life. It certainly did to mine before my trip. And yet there's much insight that we can each use to better tap into the "truth force" of stories in our everyday lives.

First, intentionality. The leaders at Standing Rock put so much thought and care into making sure the stories being created there were healing stories that united people and lifted them up, even at the moment of loss. They held space for the community to reckon with the darkness of history while daring to face the future with hope.

You can be intentional in the stories you tell as well as in the stories you consume. Examine which stories are taking your time and attention. If you're only getting information and testimony from people who look like you and sound like you, you're ultimately getting a less-than-truthful picture of the world. It takes effort to read and hear the stories of those who are invisible from our daily life. So much of our lives are still segregated in one way or another, even or especially our faith communities. As Dr. King famously said, "It is appalling that the most segregated hour of Christian America is eleven o'clock on Sunday morning."[2]

Some time ago I read a book called *The Big Sort: Why the Clustering of Like-Minded Is Tearing Us Apart* by Bill Bishop. The book centers around a statistical study of

American society at the level of zip code that shows a sad fact: America in the last decades has essentially segregated itself, not primarily along racial lines, but into communities of like-mindedness. You've got Republican-leaning zip codes, Democratic-leaning zip codes, and Independent zip codes. Apart from residential segregation, media segregates us as well. Simply put: The people who watch Sean Hannity tonight are not going to turn to MS-NBC to watch Rachel Maddow. Cable news and the rise of social media have made it possible to consume news 24/7 and never hear an opinion that differs from your own.

Now think about the consequences of communities where people simply reinforce each other's preconceived notions and ideas. When we don't have any interchange with people who have differing points of view, slowly but surely the voices of the extreme become the norm. The center, what I actually like to call the "sensible center," falls silent. And if the center does not hold, as W. B. Yeats taught us, the society will not.

We need a revival of relationships, of human relationships across difference—difference of religion, difference of ethnicity, difference of political ideology. And as former secretary of state Madeleine Albright has said, "Instead of conspiring with the like-minded, we need to spend more time learning from those we consider wrong-headed."[3]

Imagine how the world might change if people of different races, politics, or other differences met together once a week to worship—or even just to share a meal. In

2018, I hosted an Episcopal prayer breakfast for members of Congress on both side of the aisle. Democrats and Republicans came together to share prayers and conversation, and so many who attended that day commented on how rare, but wonderful, such opportunities were. But they don't need to be. We can all move in this direction. It starts with a personal commitment to seeking out relationships with people we don't know or people we think are unlike us. That can start with listening to, or reading, their stories.

Much has been made in recent years of the politics of the annual Thanksgiving table. It's a real practical conundrum for many folks, as well as a good metaphor for how to break bread with those with whom we may not agree. Some people have advised guests to confront family members who have politics or positions they believe do harm. Confrontation sounds like a great way to ruin a good turkey, not to mention destructive to the love and trust that can actually lead to personal evolution. Stories are a way to dig into politics without family members feeling attacked and on the defensive—a truth force, not a truth bomb.

I learned a powerful story-based approach to encouraging productive "across the aisle" dialogue from Charles Robinson, who is both the rector of St. Luke's in Park City, Utah, and a therapist. Charles leads a group of concerned citizens called the Project for a Deeper Understanding. Since 2006, they have hosted events where people with differing perspectives meet to discuss their most polarizing issues in a structured environment, with an audience. The focus is "deep listening" so that respectful dialogue and mutual understanding can occur. In recent years, events have been broadcast on the local radio station to take the experience to many more people.

When we met, Charles told me that when he facilitates, he likes to ask participants a question: *"For a particular issue, what is the story of your life that brought you to that conclusion?"* After a speaker finishes, Charles invites others to reflect on what they heard and understood in that person's story. This exchange of stories creates that communion of spirits. Suddenly there's a context for healing, and the possibility for a relationship, between people who were accustomed to interacting with their hackles up. No one leaves feeling like John McGraw: *We don't know who he is.*

McGraw was right. We are caught up in a political mess today, you and me, and we need to heal our country. And we can. Our stories are the song of our souls, and there is healing and hope when we hear them and share them.

CHAPTER 11

The Still More Excellent Way

Question: Does love mean avoiding politics?

> *Let us teach ourselves and others that politics*
> *can be not only the art of the possible, especially if this*
> *means the art of speculation, calculation, intrigue,*
> *secret deals and pragmatic manoeuvring, but that*
> *it can even be the art of the impossible, namely the*
> *art of improving ourselves and the world.*
> —VÁCLAV HAVEL

A FEW YEARS AGO, I helped form a group called the Reclaiming Jesus Elders. I got involved when I shared a meal with Jim Wallis, the founder of the Sojourners organization and the author of *God's Politics*. We bonded over our shared concern for the soul of Christianity in America, and also, as it happened, over a meal of soul food. In Christianity, just as in our national politics, the voices of extremists are drowning out the silent majority. And those extremists are using religion to defend a panoply of dark *isms*: racism, nationalism, nativism, sexism, and on and on. Their views don't represent the views of most Christians—but they are aggressively promoting them, to the point of crisis for the church. (I wrote as much in a foreword to Jim's book *Christ in Crisis: Reclaiming Jesus in a Fearful Time*.)

Jim drafted a declaration of core values for Christians in these times, and we worked on it together while we watched the Super Bowl and ate hot wings in the restaurant at the Capital Hilton. Leaders from more than a dozen churches signed on to become elders, together asking Christians, and Americans, to go back to the roots of their faith and reject the politics of White supremacy, racism, misogyny, and the oppression or dehumanization of anyone.

So the Reclaiming Jesus movement was born. We kicked off with a series of meetings, during which we decided we wanted to make a public witness. But what should it look like? The politics of that moment were loud, ugly, and oppositional. It was contemptuous. What could we do that wouldn't just sound like more angry shouting? We all agreed that in order to reach a peaceful, loving end, we needed a peaceful, loving means.

Many of you may be feeling the same way as you consider how to take the way of love and participate in our democracy. Our institutions are creaking and groaning under misuse and outright abuse. People are angry to the point that debate has ceased to be productive, ruled by ad hominem attacks and cruel innuendo from both sides. Some of you might have the urge to say, "I'm out. See ya." Hopefully this book has already offered a compelling defense for keeping the faith and staying engaged. But if you need more convincing, consider this: If all the decent people sit this one out, we're handing our country and our future to extremists. And while you can remove yourself from politics, you can't remove yourself from this world. If you stop paying attention, you might just find that world burning up under your feet.

We all have the same challenge: How do we *productively* engage with our democracy and our leadership so that the laws of the land reflect shared human values of compassion, mercy, and care for people and the planet? How do we follow the way of love when it comes to politics?

This question of how to engage in the public interest as religious leaders wasn't completely new to us elders. Most churches, like mine, have members from across the political spectrum. As leaders, if we want to engage the issues, we have to do it in a way that honors all the many viewpoints represented. I once got an email from a man who was angry because he thought that, shortly after the November 2016 election, his church had deliberately picked Sunday readings to criticize our new president, Donald Trump. This parishioner didn't know that those lessons were assigned in a lectionary of Bible readings for various Sundays and holy days, decided many years ago, and in some cases, centuries ago. And they repeat every three years. They are not selected according to the news cycle but according to the Good News. It turned out the readings that week happened to be the Beatitudes, Jesus's blessings from the Sermon on the Mount in Matthew's Gospel: *Blessed are the poor, blessed are the meek, blessed are the pure of heart, blessed are the peacemakers,* etc. And in those words, this man heard a critique of President Trump. The point is that we do have to be careful; people are on edge these days.

In my last few years as bishop of North Carolina I found myself compelled to become involved more directly in politics in the public square. Years before, we made an intentional decision to relocate our diocesan offices closer to our state capitol building in downtown Raleigh. I believed our presence there provided a tangible witness to the Gospel, and I wasn't being sly about it. We were *one block* from the capitol square. So I was already pretty clear about keeping close to our lawmakers, not as another interest group but as a moral and spiritual conscience.

WHEN YOU IMAGINE trying to bring *love* into political discourse, you might imagine people reacting like you're speaking an alien tongue. You might say "love your brother" and, as your answer, get punched in the face. Trying to put the two together brings to mind the famous "Grand Inquisitor" story within Fyodor Dostoyevsky's *The Brothers Karamazov,* which I read in college. (I took the course not because of my love for great literature but because I was interested in a young woman who was also taking the course. In spite of myself I actually learned something. That's been my experience of most of my learning since then. In spite of myself.)

In the story—or my version of the story, since none of the quotes below are Dostoyevsky's—Jesus returns to earth during the days of the Inquisition, when the church was seeking to convert non-Christians, Jews, and some Muslims via tribunals, arrest, and punishment. It was not a moral moment. When Jesus arrives, he doesn't get any *hosannas*. Instead, they lock him up. He goes to trial before the Grand Inquisitor, who says, "Not *you* again! You're going to ruin everything." He tells Jesus that the son of God made a big mistake way back, early in his evolution as a teacher, when the devil offered him ultimate power in exchange for fealty. Jesus said no. "Idiot!" says the Grand Inquisitor. "With ultimate power, think of all the good you could have done. Power works! Might makes right! All that love and humility and free will for humanity stuff is out. And so are you, Jesus." Apologies to Fyodor, who hopefully isn't rolling in his grave for my retelling here.

I can't speak for other religious traditions, but the further Christianity has strayed from its roots in Jesus of Nazareth—his teachings, his example, and the reality of his risen life—the more we have betrayed the one we claim to follow. The more we have remained silent or committed evils that have hurt and harmed God's creations. Dostoyevsky was right.

When the way of love becomes one's way of life, it's a game changer. It shapes every decision we make—and that changes everything, whether you're a preacher or a politician, a communist or a corporate executive, a teacher or a trash collector. And it cannot be limited to just the personal. Once it's your spiritual center of gravity, it floods every aspect and dimension of life.

Here we are in what feels like another deeply immoral moment. And again, it feels like you might get locked up by some Grand Inquisitor if you bring up all that love stuff in the context of the body politic. Truthfully, the fabled Grand Inquisitor was no dummy: Jesus was dangerous. He was a revolutionary. As my old friend from Baltimore, Professor Charles Marsh, wrote in one of his books on the spirituality of the civil rights movement: "Jesus had founded the most revolutionary movement in history: a movement built on the unconditional love of God for the world and the mandate to live that love."[1] In more recent history, proponents of slavery justified the trade using religious arguments—but they avoided Jesus like the plague. If bigotry is your game, Jesus is not the name.

Back in my days as a bishop of North Carolina, I came to realize that if we engage in politics simply on its own terms, then we join the battle royale. It's a morally self-defeating proposition. Everything becomes about power, with winners and losers, and competing ideas falsely reduced to Black and White. It's seductive, but you can't take the bait.

Let's go back one more time to the soaring words the Apostle Paul offers the unraveling Corinthian community. After he describes a church community being torn apart by unbridled self-interest and petty factionalism, he shifts gears, saying: "And I will show you a still more excellent way." He's showing them the high way, which is the way of love.

To engage productively, you first have to do what Paul did. You have to shift the conversation to higher ground— above and beyond the politics, and the issues as the players have defined them. Instead we search for values and principles that we share. In that higher moral and spiritual ground, we may find genuine common ground. When we wade back into the issues, it's from a different perspective and place.

So instead of digging in on the specific issues in North Carolina, I pulled the conversation a level higher. I said to lawmakers and advocates, "If you're making laws that impact human beings, those laws should pass the test of Jesus's Golden Rule: Do unto others as you would have them do unto you."[2] Another translation says it this way: "Treat people in the same way that you want them to treat you." Does it pass the test? If not, then let's find another humane, creative possibility.

When we came at the issue that way, we opened up conversation with people who were in very different places politically. For example, several pieces of legislation intended to loosen state regulation of inhumane working conditions for migrant workers were significantly modified, with bipartisan help. The results weren't perfect, but they were an improvement over what might have been. Some of our leaders also stepped up to change legislation that would at the time have proved harmful to Dreamers, undocumented immigrants who came here when they were children. There was one delegate in particular who had, over time, moderated some of his views on immigration. At one meeting I said to him, "You know the local news media like to cover disagreements between public religious leaders. But when Catholics, Southern Baptists, and Episcopalians are in agreement over something, that's what they should really be covering!" We laughed.

The Golden Rule itself is a great reminder that most of us share fundamental values. It's not just part of Christianity. In some form this teaching is found in most, if not all, of the world's great faith traditions. Rabbi Hillel (110 BC–AD 10), for example, taught in the Babylonian Talmud that "what is hateful to you, don't do to your fellow: this is the whole Torah; the rest is commentary; go and learn." Islam, Buddhism, Hinduism, Zoroastrianism— you name it, there's some form of the Golden Rule present in every religion I know.

I don't think that's an accident. As they sing in Alice Walker's *The Color Purple*, "God is trying to tell you something." If the New Testament is correct, as I believe it is, then the simplest, most accurate statement of who

God is and who we are meant to be may be this: "Beloved, let us love one another, because love is from God; everyone who loves is born of God and knows God. Whoever does not love does not know God, for God is love."[3]

I found myself tongue-tied before the Great Inquisitor once again two days before the presidential election in November 2016. Members of our staff said, "You need to say something to your church." We didn't know what the outcome was going to be. But we had all lived through a bitterly divisive campaign. And I didn't know what to say. I didn't want to mouth pious platitudes that said nothing. I did not want to enter the partisan fray and be either red or blue. That's not my job. But I knew I had to say something. I was stuck.

I distracted myself with a scroll through my text messages and saw a recent text from the Reverend James Oliver Lee Jr., who has been my friend since kindergarten. That's when it dawned on me to dig up my old copy of Robert Fulghum's *All I Really Need to Know I Learned in Kindergarten*, a great little book about the shared values that we teach young children. At one point he summarizes some of them:

Share everything.
Play fair.
Don't hit people.
Put things back where you found them.
Clean up your own mess.

Don't take things that aren't yours.

Say you're sorry when you hurt somebody.

Wash your hands before you eat.

Flush.

Warm cookies and cold milk are good for you.

Live a balanced life—learn some and think some and draw and paint and sing and dance and play and work every day some.

Take a nap every afternoon.

When you go out into the world, watch out for traffic, hold hands, and stick together.

The old slaves used to sing:

> *Walk together children*
> *Don't you get weary.*
> *There's a great camp meeting*
> *In the promised land.*

There it was. In the core. From there I flashed back to my first-grade teacher, Mrs. Sullivan, and I suddenly knew what to say. Later that morning I found our public affairs officer and asked her to take out her iPhone to record me. After a few introductory words, I invited us all to live by what we learned in kindergarten, our common core. And to remember what I and everybody else learned in first grade: "I pledge allegiance to the flag of the United States of America. And to the republic for which it stands,

one nation under God, indivisible, with liberty and justice for all." Peel back all the mess, and that's America.
That's who we are, and where we're going, each struggle
bringing us closer to the dream. One nation under God,
indivisible, with liberty and justice for all. All!

Love doesn't just belong in the public square; it is desperately needed there to break through deadlock and
make our diversity of perspectives an asset. Conservatives
and progressives share a number of values, and if we can
put their heads together, we can identify shared spiritual
and moral truths and values, and maybe work toward
practical solutions to our common problems.

There are some practical steps to do this.

- Identify the shared moral values and spiritual
  principles where we agree.
- Share your personal story about how those values
  and principles became important to you.
- Seek to apply those values to current challenges, and
  identify commonalities.
- Craft ways forward that best approximate those
  values and principles.

It's not rocket science. And it is true that there are
some matters on which we simply won't agree. But you
don't build on the negative. Build on the positive and on
what can be done.

There are many ways to be an instrument of love. Any

successful change movement has many contributors. We needed Martin Luther King—*and* we needed Malcolm X. Different approaches come together to move the system beyond where it is. We need everybody. But for those who truly believe in the beloved community, beloved community is what the movement to get there needs to look like.

Even more simply put, the path to love needs to look like love. For me, that means a revival of relationships, building bridges instead of trying to win points. Telling stories together. Because I believe in bridge building, I recently attended the National Prayer Breakfast. I did not, however, join the group on stage in its standing ovation after President Trump's pro-life remark.

My quiet dissent was not an earth-shattering moment. I don't know if anyone even noticed. But I needed to sit down in order to stand up for a moral conviction I believe. And that conviction was both about the immediate issue of abortion and equally about a respectful way to register dissent.

Walking love's way sometimes demands and requires standing up in public for those core values you believe are under attack. Like the Standing Rock Sioux, we can stand as protectors, not protesters, rising up to help others transcend politics and remember what's worth saving and growing and holding close.

Which brings us back to the Reclaiming Jesus Elders

and our desire to make a loving public witness. The presiding bishop of the Lutheran Church, Elizabeth Eaton, inspired the answer. She spoke of the Christians in the police state of Soviet East Germany who had started a movement of candlelight vigils through the city. The protesters walked peacefully through the streets with candles, singing hymns. It started as a few hundred faithful on the streets of Leipzig, but over time, almost the entire city was turning out with their candles. The movement spread further—and many believe it contributed to the fall of the Berlin Wall. The world saw the light of those candles, and that revolution spread.

So we planned our own candlelight vigil. We planned it thinking a thousand people would participate. The turnout was three times that. I don't think we awakened something new so much as provided an outlet that was desperately needed. There was hunger there.

On May 24, 2018, we gathered at Washington's National City Christian Church. The mood of the crowd felt calm but solemn as we stepped out into the warm evening. A snapshot of that day's news events speaks volumes about the moment in history: An Oklahoma man opened fire in a local restaurant. Our forty-fifth president, in a television interview, said that NFL players who took a knee during the national anthem to protest police brutality and racial oppression maybe "shouldn't be in the country."[4] And film producer Harvey Weinstein surrendered himself to the authorities on sex assault charges while denying he broke the law.

But also in the news of that day was the Reclaiming Jesus prayer vigil. We were lucky: Though the event had been planned months before, the timing was great. Just one week prior, I had been on TVs all over the world preaching at the royal wedding. More folks—and media outlets—than usual were interested in what Michael Curry was up to, so the evening was widely covered.

Together we walked, mostly in silence, sometimes singing, thousands of us slowly traveling the handful of blocks from the church to the White House. When we got there, we waited patiently to be allowed into the area outside the gate surrounding the lawn. Once they let us enter, the group gathered together, a great throng of people with glowing candles. Next to the gates, the elders walked in a circle with posters that reproduced our declaration. I prayed, my voice amplified by a bullhorn, that God would guide and direct the leaders of the nations of the earth, and the peoples of our country, to do what is just, what is merciful, while walking humbly.

The turnout that night showed me, once again, that so many people want to model another way of being for the world. To be witnesses not so much to any religion but to their faith that we live in a world where human kindness, compassion, and justice for all will prevail, because it is God's way. Of course, we were also pointedly witnessing to those values while standing a few hundred yards of green lawn away from where they were being mocked, inside the White House, where all but one of our forty-five American presidents have lived and led.

People wanted to call the White House action a protest, but I was adamant: It was prayer, not protest. We weren't there to wave fingers at our president or anyone else. We were there to declare our own beliefs and to pray with open hearts for our leadership. We were there to seek higher ground and discover common ground. We were not protesters but protectors of Jesus's way of love.

Before the vigil began, we had held a worship service inside the great church. Each of the elders spoke. When I had the floor, I said this:

> We are not a partisan group. We are not a left-wing group. We are not a right-wing group. We are a Jesus movement. That's who we are. And we came together, Protestant, Catholic, and evangelical. We came together, Republicans, Independents, and Democrats. We came together, liberal, conservative, and whatever is in the middle. We came together because what binds us together is Jesus of Nazareth and his way and his teaching and his life.
>
> And when we leave this place, in silent prayerful vigil, walking together to the White House, let it be known that this is not a protest march. This is a procession of Christian people. This is what they did on Pentecost. This is a Pentecostal moment. That's what's going on.

We are committed to following the way of Jesus. And when that lawyer asked Jesus, what is the great law in the law of Moses? Jesus answered, reaching back to the Hebrew Scriptures and quoting the teaching of Moses: "You shall love the Lord your God with all your heart, all your soul, all your mind. This is the first and great commandment."

But the second is just like it: "You shall love your neighbor as yourself." Love your neighbor—that's why we are here. Love the neighbor you like and love the neighbor you don't like. Love the neighbor you agree with and love the neighbor you disagree with. Love your Democrat neighbor. Love your Republican neighbor. Love your Independent neighbor. Love your Black neighbor, your White neighbor. Love your Asian neighbor, your Latino neighbor, and your Indigenous neighbor. Love your South American neighbor. Love your LGBTQ neighbor, love your Jewish neighbor, love your Muslim neighbor. Love, love, love, love your neighbor as yourself. On these two hang all the law and the prophets.

All the law and the prophets. Everything God has been trying to lay out for us. Everything the Bible and sacred texts around the world have been straining to say. As Duke Ellington sang, "It don't mean a thing if it ain't got that swing." Or to make it plain, if it's not about love, it's not about God. And if it is about love, then it is about God.

I know that all of us are a mixed-up collection of selfish interests and selfless impulses, but I believe most people are fundamentally decent. As folk used to say, "There's a little bit of bad in the best of us and a little bit of good in the worst of us." We are complex. But I believe that most of us are capable of kindness and inclined toward altruism if given a chance.

It has also been said, "The only thing necessary for the triumph of evil is for good men to do nothing." We need good and kind and decent people to rise up and stand up for that which is loving, that which is kind, that which is compassionate, and that which is just, merciful, and humane. Let no one be deceived: Kindness is not weakness any more than love is a whimsical sentiment.

Love is powerful, transformative, free, and freeing to all.

Dr. King was right: "We must discover the power of love, the power, the redemptive power of love. And when we discover that, we will be able to make of this old world a new world. Love is the only way."[5]

CHAPTER 12

Hope, Help, and Healing

THE WAY OF love is a commitment to seeking the good and well-being of others. When we truly do that, we all are blessed. In fact, if we all made the commitment—to loving beyond our nationality, our ethnicity, our politics, our religion, or any other difference—we and the earth itself would be blessed.

Some years ago, I was flying from Nairobi, Kenya, to Bujumbura, Burundi. The flight pattern took us near Tanzania's great Mount Kilimanjaro. I was reading a book and almost missed seeing it. Fortunately I was flying with Bishop Rob O'Neill of Colorado. From the seat behind, he tapped me on the shoulder and said, "Sorry to disturb you from your reading, but look out the window." I did, and there, reaching up to us, was the snowcapped peak of Kilimanjaro.

My jaw dropped. I felt that shiver down my spine. And

I remembered the words of one of my grandmother's favorite hymns, "Then sings my soul, my Savior God to thee. How great thou art, how great thou art."

There is something about mountains, the sheer majesty of their shape and size, rising out of the earth and yet seemingly greater than the earth, or even alien to it. Mountaintops cause the jaw to drop and the soul to wonder.

Ancient folk knew this strange quality. The Celts called mountaintops "thin places," where heaven and earth seem to touch. As I see it, a thin place can be a moment or an experience as much as a place. It's those times when your jaw drops and words don't rise to the occasion. This world is touched by another. Human beings encounter the divine. We experience God.

That is why, I suspect, mountains and mountaintops are often holy places in the Bible. It was on a mountain volcano called Sinai that Moses encountered God, who commanded him to lead Hebrew slaves to freedom. It was on that same mountain years later that Moses received the sublime gift of the Decalogue, the Ten Commandments. It was on a mountain that the New Testament places Jesus teaching the way of love in what is often called the Sermon on the Mount. And in the night before his martyrdom, Dr. King spoke of ultimate hope in the biblical language of the mountaintop and promised land. On mountaintops, prophets and poets see what the Bible calls "a new heaven and a new earth," a new humanity, the beloved community, the human family of God.

IN 2001, I visited a sacred mountaintop, though I didn't see it coming when The Episcopal Church extended the invitation. Along with two hundred others, I spent a weekend at the Kanuga Conference Center, high up in the mountains of North Carolina. Looking at the assembled group, you'd be hard-pressed to guess what brought us together. Among us were drag queens, heavily tattooed motorcyclists, and corporate executives. There were people from the city and people from the country. Some of us were religious, some not. We represented every color and stripe of humanity in the United States.

And yet, what we experienced together, if just for the twinkling of an eye, was a vision of the promised land, where we sat in beloved community, as the human family of God.

The Church had brought us together in a weekend retreat for people with HIV and AIDS, along with their families, loved ones, and caregivers. It was to be a weekend of sabbath for spiritual and personal renewal and revival, a time devoted to being with God and with each other.

I had been invited to offer a couple of meditations Friday night and Saturday morning, and a sermon for the healing service on Saturday evening. I used the words of the old slave spiritual "Balm in Gilead" as the text and song for the weekend. The song is a response to Jeremiah's cry in the Bible:

> My joy is gone; grief is upon me;
> my heart is sick within me . . .
> "The harvest is past, the summer is ended,
> and we are not saved." . . .
> I mourn, and dismay has taken hold on me.
> Is there no balm in Gilead?[1]

The slaves in America knew what Jeremiah was talking about. They had been ripped from their African homeland, carted on ships as cargo, and sold like cattle, children separated from parents, families torn apart never to see each other again.

They heard Jeremiah's cry. They knew his suffering. And miraculously across centuries, oceans, and cultures, they felt community with his suffering, and answered him with hope. Yes, Jeremiah, there *is* a balm in Gilead, to make the wounded whole:

> Sometimes I feel discouraged,
> And think my work's in vain,
> But then the Holy Spirit
> Revives my soul again.
>
> If you cannot sing like angels,
> If you can't preach like Paul,

You can tell the love of Jesus,
And say He died for all.

Sickness and suffering had occasioned our gathering at Kanuga. But it was love that lifted us up and brought us together. At the healing service where I gave this sermon, the warmth radiated from and to every person there. We could feel an energy not our own, the very spirit of God filling the place. For a moment, our egos fell away, and with them, our differences. We experienced ourselves as friendly souls, free and whole and beloved.

We were on the mountaintop. Love did that then, and love can do that for us now, in our country and in every country.

NOT TOO LONG AGO I found myself invited again to the mountaintop—and again, I didn't see it coming. I was making a pastoral visit for a church convention in one of our dioceses in the Southwest. The day concluded with a banquet at which I was the speaker. Afterward, I was receiving people one by one for brief conversations and selfies. Among the people in line, I noticed a bearded man in casual clothes towering over the others. He had to be at least six feet five. And while everyone else was smiling, chattering, and holding smartphones for their selfies, he was solitary and serious. I couldn't read his expression, but it was clear that he was experiencing the moment dif-

ferently from those around him. I felt my "danger anten-
nae" twitch but did nothing.

When he came closer, I could see his eyes. They were
somewhat red; was he angry or had he cried?

When he reached me, I was slightly wary, but he immediately extended his large, open hand. "I'm so glad that
you're my bishop and that you're my brother," he said.

He told me his story. He had grown up with a father
and grandfather who called themselves Christians but
were leaders in the Ku Klux Klan. But he had left home
for college, then moved to a small town in Arkansas. While
there, he wandered into a small Episcopal church in town,
even though (or perhaps because) it was not the church of
his upbringing.

As time went on, he got to know the people in this little
church well enough to share his family story, which was
still a source of great pain. And then he said, "And they
loved me anyway." They taught him about the God who
loves unconditionally, and helped him find the truth of
his faith. They healed him.

Brothers! Siblings! Children of God! They are everywhere, in all disguises. Before he left me, we embraced,
and there we were: On the mountaintop! He took me there.
And in turn, his church had taken him there. Somewhere
in the Ozark Mountains of Arkansas, some people in a
little church in a little place had showed love to a stranger.
They did so likely not expecting anything in return. They
probably don't know the full impact of their love on this

gentleman. And yet they became witnesses to the power of love to lift us to the mountaintop, where humans can dance with God's dream. Their loved changed his world, and our world with it.

Love does that! We can't live on the mountaintop, but the mountaintop can live in us.

When God, who is love, becomes our spiritual center of gravity, and love our moral compass, we live differently, regardless of what the world around us does. The world changes for the better, one life at a time.

So don't give up on love.

Listen to it.

Trust it.

Give into it.

Obey it.

Love can help and heal when nothing else can. Love can lift up and liberate when nothing else will. May God love you and bless you. And may God hold us all in those almighty hands of love.

Appendix

Love in Action—a Daily Planner

So much that's happening in the world today doesn't look like love. If we go through life letting external forces—our news feeds, our acquaintances, our Google calendar—determine how our days are spent and our contributions measured, we know what we're going to get: more of the same.

To live into our faith and values, we need to bring intentionality and purpose to every day—and that's where what's called a *rule of life* comes in to support us. Note my language: It *supports* us. It's not there to constrain you or punish you. It's not going to hit you with a ruler when you're bad. "Rule" is from the Latin *regula*, which suggests a gentle pattern or framework—not a hard and fast rule. This is a way to create tangible habits that support our heart's intentions.

The concept is an ancient one, with Christian monastic origins. The most famous rule of life is St. Benedict's, which has guided Benedictine monks for fifteen centuries. When St. Benedict and the early monks retreated from society to devote their lives to God, they walked into the desert. It was a literal and figurative void. They found caves or other natural structures to live in, but when it came to their daily actions, they needed to create structure from scratch. Devoting yourself to God sounds good, but it's completely abstract. To live it, as a flesh and blood human, a question's got to be answered: What are you going to *do* all day?

Benedict's answer took the form of a seventy-three-chapter rule of life that functioned almost like a constitution for the monks who followed his path. It created an accountable community where shared vows took life in a ritual of daily actions, balanced between prayer and work.

Rest easy: You're not renouncing modern life. You don't need seventy-three chapters. Your rule of life will be much simpler and fit your own circumstances. The Episcopal Church has created one model that we call the Way of Love: Practices for a Jesus-Centered Life.[1] I'm going to walk you through creating your own here. Feel free to work through the process at length in a journal or on a computer, but have the goal of producing a final version that fits on a single sheet of paper. Then print it out and keep it somewhere prominent.

The process here is designed to be used for readers of any faith or spiritual inclination to grow closer to the God who is love, however you define that, and closer to our truest, most loving self.

TIPS TO GET STARTED

- Be realistic. You do you. This isn't about becoming a perfect version of yourself, or about achieving someone else's idea of the right way to live. This is about living more fully in values you already hold by building some habits that fit comfortably into your regular life.
- Be loving. Don't turn this exercise into a catalog of regrets or self-criticism. Work from a gentle acceptance of where you are, and give yourself some love for taking time for spiritual development.
- Don't wait! Dive in right away. But pick an annual date to revise your rule of life, during the time of year that you customarily reflect on your life journey. Your rule of life will change over time, and so will you.

Steps for Creating Your Rule of Life

1. Identify one to three core values or principles that you would like to live more deeply into. Consider your own experience: What values drive the people you most love or admire? What might most contribute to your growth?

St. Benedict's vows have proved remarkably resilient, so we'll use them as examples: obedience, silence, and humility. They get even more interesting with some interpretation.

Obedience comes from the Latin *obidere*, "to listen." Who among us couldn't work on being a more careful listener? Understood spiritually, you might work toward listening to hear where the spirit is calling you—and making changes accordingly.

Silence, for monks, is sometimes a literal vow. But silence can also be understood as saying less or applying restraint to the words you say. Are your words loving? Are they contributing productively to conversation with your family members, neighbors, and colleagues? Silence could stand for aligning the things you say with the values you hold dear.

Humility is the commitment to selfless living, to judging your actions according to whether they contribute to the common good. Humility is the shift from *me* to *we*.

2. Use the value(s) you chose to write vows that summarize what the values specifically mean in the context of your life and your reason for wanting to translate them into changes to your daily life. For example, you might write, *I vow to spend more time listening to others than I have in the past, for better understanding and to find better, more loving solutions for the common good.*

3. Now brainstorm some habits that will allow you to practice the values you identified in various areas of your life. Look around and look at the stories of wise ones who came before to see what others have practiced. Below are some recommended categories to consider. Don't feel that you have to explore each one; instead, consider which are the most important for your life and your values. For each category that resonates, design one to three habits that will allow you to live your mission statement more fully.

4. While using a daily, weekly, or monthly calendar to create regular habits works for many, don't be afraid to create a schedule that fits your personal schedule. For example, when I was a parish priest, I scheduled one day a week as my day for reading, study, and reflection. As presiding bishop, I don't have that kind of schedule freedom, but I do spend a lot of time on airplanes. Now I commit a portion of my in-flight time to reading and reflection.

Categories for Action

BODY: How can you put yourself in the best physical and mental state to live into your vows? Examples might be to commit to daily movement, schedule an annual doctor's visit, take days off when you're sick, or see a therapist regularly.

MIND: Commit to time for growth, learning, and enrichment that support your vows. To carve out that time, is there social media or screen time that you might eliminate? For example, you might commit to thirty minutes of bedtime reading and reduce social media use or TV time accordingly.

SPIRIT: Commit to a regular schedule of prayer, meditation, or rituals that offer freedom from the self, to connect with God and the greater universe. Examples might be saying grace or expressing gratitude at mealtimes with your family, praying or meditating daily, attending a weekly gathering of your faith community, or spending time in nature or in solitude.

RELATIONSHIPS: What practices would allow you to strengthen your most important relationships? Examples might include entering couples' counseling with your partner, saying "I love you" to someone every day, or weekly quality time with your partner, children, or other loved ones.

GIVING BACK: Commit to sharing your resources of time, money, or attention with others. Ask yourself, *Where will my presence be most healing? What resources do I have to offer those in need?* Examples might include committing to a monthly nonprofit donation, tithing 10 percent of your income to give to others, or signing up to volunteer with a local organization.

COMMUNITY: Where can you find and join like-minded people who could support you over time in practicing your rule of life? Consider the question for all the categories above.

Please Don't Walk Alone

Change isn't easy. Every single person on earth who's ever tried to do the right thing—the self-honoring thing, the selfless thing—with any consistency, struggles. Whether you're a banker or a bishop or a boxer, we all struggle.

The most essential truth I've learned in my own journey is that none of us has the capacity to walk it alone. We need help from the very source of these principles— from God's love. And we also need soul companions to help us along the way.

I know I'm in the church business, and it may sound like I'm trying to drum up business. I'm not. I just believe with all my heart and soul that we need a power that's greater than ours and an angle of vision that is greater. We need spiritual energy, the source of love that is bottomless and endless. And then, we need each other.

Acknowledgments

The West African proverb "It takes a village to raise a child," may be well-worn, but it's also true. It quite literally takes a village, and not just to raise a child. Adults need their village, too. "No man is an island entire unto itself," wrote John Donne. We are products of our environment, offspring of the people whose lives have influenced us, and children of the God who created us all. That has most certainly been true in my life, and true in the life of this book as it came to be.

For all who are listed here, I thank them, and I thank God for them.

For Sara Grace, who has been a real partner in this effort, asking probing questions, eliciting translation of meanings from church language into world language, coaching, and co-writing.

For Merrilee Heifetz, my incredible literary agent; Rebecca, who supports and assists her; and all the folk at

Writers House who have guided me through the world of writing and publishing.

For Paul Levitz, author, editor, and former president and publisher of DC Comics, who took an interest in this message about love and introduced me to Merrilee and the Writers House team.

For the miracle-working team at Avery: Megan Newman, Nina Shield, Hannah Steigmeyer, and Anne Kosmoski, who have guided and made possible this book, as well as my previous book on the power and way of love.

For remarkable colleagues and co-workers who have helped in the conception and birth of this and my previous work on love. For the Reverend Canon Chuck Robertson and the Reverend Stephanie Spellers, who nurtured the project all along the way, from proposal to reading and critiquing the near-final manuscript. For Sharon Jones, my executive assistant and coordinator, who has coordinated virtually every meeting and deadline needed to make it happen.

For those colleagues who read the near-final manuscript and offered helpful suggestions: Mary Kostel, chancellor to the Presiding Bishop; the Reverend Canon Mark Stevenson; Nancy Davidge; Robert Wright; and finally, Bishop Michael Hunn, who quite literally prayed this book into being.

For members of the leadership team who have been supportive throughout this process: the Reverend Gay Clarke Jennings, the Reverend Canon Michael Barlowe, treasurer and CFO Kurt Barnes, the Reverend Deacon Geof Smith, COO, and Douglas Anning, interim chief legal officer, in addition to the three canons mentioned above.

For the Episcopal congregations and faith communities I have been blessed to serve and be a part of, and who have profoundly influenced and formed me: St. Simon of Cyrene in Maywood, Illinois, where I was born and baptized as a baby; St. Philip's Church in Buffalo, New York, where I, with generations of young people, grew up; St. Luke's and St. Paul's Churches in New Haven, Connecticut; and Epiphany Church in Rocky Mount, North Carolina, where I was a seminarian intern. For those congregations where I served as a pastor: St. Stephen's in Winston-Salem, North Carolina; St. Simon of Cyrene in Lincoln Heights, Ohio; and St. James Church in Baltimore, Maryland. For the Episcopal Diocese of North Carolina, where I served as bishop, and The Episcopal Church, where I serve as presiding bishop.

Last, but not least, to the source of life and love, God, who is the creator of us all and who has made us the children of God, meant to be God's human family. In the love that makes that possible is our hope.

Notes

Introduction

1. **We must learn to live:** © 1964 Dr. Martin Luther King, Jr., copyright © renewed 1992 Coretta Scott King.
2. **In my Father's house:** John 13:17.

Chapter 1: What Is This Thing Called Love?

1. **Dr. King referred to this:** © 1962 Dr. Martin Luther King, Jr., copyright © renewed 1990 Coretta Scott King.
2. **No one has greater love:** John 15:13.

Chapter 3: Making Do and Making New

1. **Black cooks had no choice:** Adrian Miller, *Soul Food: The Surprising Story of an American Cuisine, One Plate at a Time* (Chapel Hill: UNC Press, 2013), p. 265.
2. **Yet, O Lord, you are our Father:** Isaiah 64:8.
3. **Let love be genuine:** Romans 12:9–21.
4. **I have learned the secret:** Philippians 4:12–13.
5. **Langston Hughes, "Mother to Son"** from *The Collected Poems of Langston Hughes* by Langston Hughes, edited by Arnold Rampersad with David Roessel, Associate Editor, copyright © 1994 by the Estate of Langston Hughes. Used by permission of Alfred A.

Knopf, an imprint of the Knopf Doubleday Publishing Group, a division of Penguin Random House LLC. All rights reserved, and by permission of Harold Ober Associates.

Chapter 4: What Desmond Tutu and Dolly Parton Have in Common

1. **What happens to a dream:** "What happens to a dream deferred? . . . Or does it explode?" from *The Collected Poems of Langston Hughes* by Langston Hughes, edited by Arnold Rampersad with David Roessel, Associate Editor, copyright © 1994 by the Estate of Langston Hughes. Used by permission of Alfred A. Knopf, an imprint of the Knopf Doubleday Publishing Group, a division of Penguin Random House LLC. All rights reserved, and by permission of Harold Ober Associates.
2. **Dr. King often said:** © 1965 Dr. Martin Luther King, Jr., copyright © renewed 1993 Coretta Scott King.
3. **Mighty waters cannot quench:** Song of Solomon 8:7.
4. **Hold fast to dreams:** "Dreams" from *The Collected Poems of Langston Hughes* by Langston Hughes, edited by Arnold Rampersad with David Roessel, Associate Editor, copyright © 1994 by the Estate of Langston Hughes. Used by permission of Alfred A. Knopf, an imprint of the Knopf Doubleday Publishing Group, a division of Penguin Random House LLC. All rights reserved, and by permission of Harold Ober Associates.
5. **Ten Commandments of Nonviolence:** © 1963 Dr. Martin Luther King, Jr., copyright © renewed 1991 Coretta Scott King.

Chapter 5: Love's Call—and Love's Calling

1. **I certainly don't want:** Lynn Rosellini, "The First of the 'Mitered Mamas,'" *U.S. News & World Report*, June 19, 1989.
2. **One way to help combat:** *Michael Curry and Barbara Harris, In Conversation,* ed. Fredrica Harris Thompsett (New York: Church Publishing, 2017), p. 60.
3. **So say the Asian:** "On the Pulse of Morning" from *On the Pulse of the Morning* by Maya Angelou, copyright © 1993 by Random

Chapter 6: It's Not Easy

1. **If there is no struggle:** Frederick Douglass, "West India Emancipation," speech delivered at Canandaigua, New York, August 4, 1857.—*The Life and Writings of Frederick Douglass*, ed. Philip S. Foner, vol. 2, p. 437 (1950).
2. **We may never see the end results:** Prayer by Bishop Ken Untener of Saginaw, for a homily by Cardinal John Dearden in November 1979; commonly misattributed to the former archbishop of San Salvador Óscar Romero, who shared the philosophy but never spoke the words.
3. **I am the Lord your God:** Exodus 20:2–3.
4. **I planted, Apollos watered:** 1 Corinthians 3:6.

Chapter 7: Leave No One Behind

1. **Stay in the city:** Luke 24:49.

Chapter 8: When The Spirit Reworks You

1. **the heart is devious:** Jeremiah 17:9.
2. **I press toward the mark:** Philippians 3:14.

Chapter 9: The Real E Pluribus Unum

1. **Walk in love:** Ephesians 5:2.
2. **All who have been baptized:** Galatians 3:28.

Chapter 10: The Great Relationship Revival

1. **If I met you in the street:** "Clash at Trump Rally Ends in Probation, Handshake," WRAL.com, December 14, 2016, https://www.wral.com/clash-at-trump-rally-ends-in-probation-handshake/16339805/.

2. **As Dr. King famously said:** © 1960 Dr. Martin Luther King, Jr., copyright © renewed 1988 Coretta Scott King.

3. **Instead of conspiring with the like-minded:** Madeleine K. Albright, *Madam Secretary: A Memoir* (New York: Miramax, 2003), p. 663.

Chapter 11: The Still More Excellent Way

1. **Jesus had founded the most revolutionary:** Charles Marsh, *The Beloved Community: How Faith Shapes Social Justice, from the Civil Rights Movement to Today* (New York: Basic Books, 2005), p. 81.

2. **If you're making laws:** Luke 6:31.

3. **"Beloved, let us love one another:** 1 John 4:7–8.

4. **shouldn't be in the country:** Donald Trump on *Fox and Friends*, interview by Brian Kilmeade, aired May 24, 2018, Fox News.

5. **Dr. King was right:** © 1957 Dr. Martin Luther King, Jr., copyright © renewed 1985 Coretta Scott King.

Chapter 12: Hope, Help, and Healing

1. **My joy is gone:** Jeremiah 8:18-22.

Appendix: Love in Action—a Daily Planner

1. **Way of Love:** "The Way of Love: Practices for a Jesus-Centered Life," The Episcopal Church, www.episcopalchurch.org/wayoflove.